HOW TO PREPARE FOR THE JOURNEY:
VOLUME II

The

Sea of Faces

BY AL MINER AND LAMA SING

The Sea of Faces – How to Prepare for the Journey: Vol II
Copyright ©2006 by Al and Susan Miner

2nd Edition 2017

Cover art and book design by Susan M. Miner

ISBN-13 978-0-9791262-1-5
1. Lama Sing 2. Psychics 3. Trance Channel 4. Death and Dying
I. Miner, Al   II. Title

Library of Congress Control Number: 2006909909

Printed in the United States of America

For books and products, further information, or to write Al Miner visit
www.lamasing.org

In meditation, when moving through other realms of consciousness, you may have noticed on occasion any number of faces observing you. Often in great number, they are outside the Tunnel of Light, in which a person often travels from one state of consciousness to another. Somewhere back in the eighties I coined the phrase 'the Sea of Faces' to describe the very impressive array of faces looking back at me as I was moving in Consciousness.

–Al Miner

EXCERPT: "The Sea of Faces is primarily comprised of souls bound to the Earth by their desires, usually carnal... often those involved in influencing other souls who have abandoned their free will, their hope, their purpose, or who are in some way addicted. All must pass through this 'Sea' in one manner or another in the movement out of the finite dimension of Earth consciousness... the passage which you call Death."

–Lama Sing

TABLE OF CONTENTS

Editor's Notes:

With the exception of a few words here and there, what you are about to read are the words of Lama Sing given in separate sessions (called readings), channeled by Al Miner. Questions that were sent in by the sponsor were read by Al at the opening, after which he placed himself into the trance state. Lama Sing would then enter the dimension of Earth, borrowing Al's voice for the reading.

Even though the name Lama Sing has been assigned to these readings, there is actually always a group involved. Depending upon the topic, sometimes the number is massive, and sometimes it is a handful; sometimes they are speaking to a group, and sometimes to an individual they know will one day get the message – in essence, speaking to one and all, as well as to only one and only all... curious, but true. Throughout the reading, they defer to one another just as we do when in a group discussion. This information may be of value as you read, so you don't stumble when they sometimes change, even in a single paragraph, from an archaic form of speech to a more modern one, or from the singular to the plural.

The name Channel is used by Lama Sing in place of Al, because to use the name Al would essentially serve to call him – call him from that consciousness to which he is taken that prevents his personal involvement and influence in what is given in the reading. There is only one known occasion in which Lama Sing used Al's given name. The reason given was that the depth of his channeled state was being tested.

Lastly...

There are places where Lama Sing emphasizes a thought by speaking the words quote/end-quote. To let the reader know that those emphases are Lama Sing's, as opposed to the transcriber's, the words quote/end-quote have been kept in the text as well as the quotation marks themselves.

The word dis-ease is used by Lama Sing to mean, not only illness and such, but "first and foremost, a lack of ease in spirit, mind, and/or emotion, which are then precipitated into the physical body."

Lama Sing's use of words such as ye, thee, whom, and he is often contrary to conventional, but the meaning will be clear.

Forward: A Message from Al

Before I came into this work, I'd never heard of anything like the Sea of Faces. Then one day in a journey to do a reading, as I was floating upwards in the beautiful translucent tunnel of light, I happened to look outside the tunnel and was stunned to see a face looking back at me.

The longer I worked as a channel, the more faces there were, almost as though my channeling work was attracting them like moths to a flame, and the more comfortable I became with their presence. Some seemed to simply be curious about who I was and what I was doing there. Others cried out to me pitifully, with an impact on me that was difficult to resist. Others were arrogant, even trying to command me to do this or that. Finally, there were those who were simply vile.

After studying thousands of faces like that, it's easy to recognize the ones who are sincere in their curiosity, who just don't seem to belong there. On one occasion, I became aware of a little group of entities moving upwards with me, peering at me the whole time. Through the wall of filamental luminosity, like a living sheer curtain, I was looking at them and they were looking at me, probably not more than four feet away, a curious innocence or sweetness to them. One fellow reached out tentatively, as we were all moving up, and like someone testing the temperature of water, he put his hand out and touched the Tunnel of Light. When he touched the tunnel, it felt like he was touching me! Instantly, beings of light appeared all around his group.

When the fellow saw the beings of light, he began to weep and said something like, "I don't want to stay here anymore. Please, take me with you." He and several others were sort of embraced by those beings of light, and whoosh—they were gone. They never came into the tunnel with me. I guess because it was my tunnel, my life force. Some of those in the back or on the periphery of that group, though... I don't know whether they were frightened or what... but they slowly moved backwards into the darkness, until I could no longer see them. After what seemed to be a great deal of time but was probably only moments, there was no one on the other side of the tunnel anymore and I began to move upwards again very quickly. But it left me with a melancholy feeling, because I couldn't stop thinking about the ones who had moved back into the darkness—what are they doing now, what's happening to them?

On another journey through the tunnel, I noticed a face, and the warmth of familiarity touched me, so I paused. What if you, in your journey to the beyond, happen to see a familiar face peering at you, beckoning to you from the Sea of Faces. What if it is the face of someone you have loved or a dear friend, what would you do? Would you take their out-stretched hand and join them in their realm of limitation? My experience with the familiar face went something like this:

Face: "I've been waiting for you! It's been so long. I am so happy you've come to join me!"

Me: "Uh-h-h, I haven't come to join you, I'm just passing through. But tell me, why are you here in this place?"

Face: "I died, remember? And this is where I came to. I'm quite happy here, but part of me is lonely for something… someone… and when I saw you just a moment ago, I remembered you. Something inside me wants to be with you! Please, come stay with me here!"

Me: "I can't do that. I still have a life on Earth. I'm just traveling to meet my friends to do a reading."

Face: "What's a reading, and where are you going?"

Me: "I'm going off to get information for someone on Earth… you know… psychic stuff."

Face: "You mean that stuff is real?"

Me: "Yes"

Face: "Where do you go to get the information?"

Me: "Someplace beautiful where everyone is at peace and joyful. Why don't you come with me?"

Face: "I couldn't do that, I have penance to do."

Me: "Penance to whom? For what?"

Face: "For things I did in my life before I died."

Me: "Tell me, do you feel dead?"

Face: "No… but I'm not ready to face God yet."

Me: "Why don't you just come with me. If you don't like it there, I'll be returning in an hour or so and I'll bring you back here. And… I promise you won't have to face God, if you don't want to," smiling brightly.

Face: "Really? You promise?"

Me: "I promise."

Off we went to see the Lama Sing group. "Face" was so overwhelmed with joy and freedom, he began to laugh and dance. Of course we all joined him. He never came back to the Sea of Faces. Where he went, I don't recall, but the last I saw him, he was arm-in-arm with several others, singing as they moved off into the light.

Some of the beings appear so incredibly sweet, and reach out to me with such poignancy that it takes everything that I can muster to not stop. They may call out something like, "Oh sir! Could you just help me for a moment or two, please?" If I respond with something like, "I'll be glad to send someone to help you but I can't stop, I have to go on," sometimes they'd transform into something heinous, and start cursing at me as I passed by. Whenever one in the Sea of Faces truly wants out, they need only ask, and someone from the Light is immediately there, to help them move on. So I came to realize that such pleas were insincere at best, and at worst were just another attempt to get me to move off my path and into their realm—they don't really want your help, they want you!

After I'd been working for many years, there were fewer and fewer faces. I guess it became sort of like, "Oh it's just that guy again. He goes up and down all the time." I guess they gave up trying to lure me, as though they knew they weren't going to get me, so why bother.

What is our point of revealing the Sea of Faces to the Earth? Everyone in the process of leaving through the doorway called death will move through the Sea of Faces. Some will have an intimate awareness of every step of that movement through. For the majority, however, the journey through will only be a flash of an array of emotions and in the equivalent of the blink of an eye, it will be gone; what will follow next will be the Light, the peace, and those things that are of the higher intent of that soul. Hundreds of thousands, perhaps millions, are stuck in the Sea of Faces, but it is by their choice! Knowing about the choice empowers you to move through it with ease.

Knowing about the Sea of Faces can also empower your life while on Earth. Wherever there is conflict, hostility, activities of darkness, entities from the Sea are right there. If one holds an attitude of hatred, others from the Sea are there fueling the hatred, and the object of the hatred is being encouraged all the more by what is being contributed to it, so that what may have begun as a thought of anger, when nourished by these entities, can result in out-and-out conflict. Those in the Sea of Faces cannot interact physically but they can interact with our thoughts and emotions. Likewise, wherever there are positive, loving, light-filled thoughts, those of the Light are there immediately, and they use that energy to further the light in the world. Today's thoughts are tomorrow's actions and results.

Finally, by knowing about the Sea of Faces, we are informed of one of the foremost works before us all—to set free every last one of those souls dwelling there. If you wish to help, you can do so through your prayer and meditation and the way in which you live your life, which nurtures mass-mind thought here and beyond with the light and beauty of who you are.

As I leave you to explore with Lama Sing the depth and nature of the Sea of Faces, I offer this thought... there will one day come for you that wondrous time when you will lay aside your physical body and be welcomed "home" by great beings of light. It will be a very precious time for you... perhaps one of the most precious for you in all of your eternity. It would be my encouragement that when that time comes for you to release life on Earth for your life beyond, that you not pause to answer a call or to be otherwise lured off your path, but that you treasure that moment for the gift it is intended to be for you, to be lifted into the light and into the waiting arms of those who love and have missed you.

–Al Miner

And so, Father, we prayerfully submit this request now to you, asking as we do that you would guide us to that information that you know to be the very best, that we might be better enabled to understand this topic and the individuals or entities who are, for the most part, I guess we could say, "trapped" in this realm. And perhaps that would help us to help them, by understanding. We ask this of you in the name of the Master, The Christ, and we thank you, Father, for this and all the other blessings that we have in each and every day. Amen.

–Al Miner

As we commence with these works, let us join together in this humble prayer.

O Father-Mother-God, we know of Thee in the spirit of all that is good. We see in this goodness a light, and we know that light to be an eternal one which is constantly flowing from Thee and to we. And so, too, then, do we know of this in the spirit of those works which go before the needs of all of those who have lost their way. And it is unto that intent, Father, that we seek herein to provide just a whit more of Thy light unto those who are willing to receive same. We pray of Thee, Father, that Thou would grant us the presence of the Master, The Christ, in these works, so as to impart His healing grace, love, compassion, and wisdom unto all those who are gathered and those whom shall follow. This prayer and its intent of light do we offer, as well, on behalf of all those souls in all realms who are presently dwelling in the darkness of their own illusion, and for whom there are none in joyful prayer. Humbly we thank Thee, Father, for this continued opportunity of joyous service in Thy name. So let it be written. Amen.

–Lama Sing

Part One:

Exploring The Sea of Faces

READING 1: EARTHBOUND

AL MINER/CHANNEL: This is February 12, 1998. This is a request for a topical research reading titled "The Sea of Faces".

What is the Sea of Faces

I think it would be well for me to briefly define to those who are not familiar with this term how we came to use it and how we first became aware of it. In meditation or experiences wherein you feel that you are moving through other levels or realms of consciousness, you may have noticed on occasion that you will see an array of faces observing you.

Often these are great in number, and they—in my experience and the experience of friends and associates—are seen often outside of the (as it's called) Tunnel of Light, in which a person often travels from one state of consciousness to another.

So, somewhere back in time I coined the phrase "the Sea of Faces" to describe the very impressive array of faces looking back at us as we were moving in consciousness. I know that's not a very complete description, but perhaps it will help a little if you are not familiar with that term.

Here are the questions I've been given for this reading:

QUESTIONS

Lama Sing, this is a topical reading on the Sea of Faces.

Please start by describing the Sea of Faces?

What is it? Who inhabits it?

Why were they drawn to that realm?

What did they do/not do, to become inhabitants there?

How long do they stay? How do they finally "graduate"?

Do they gather for any conscious growth experiences,

1

like spiritual classes? Or are they in an ocean of mundane desires, with little desire for spiritual growth?

Do the entities in the Sea of Faces have guides? Where are they? What are they doing?

What does prayer from the Earth do for an entity in the Sea of Faces? Is it true that an entity can be kept out of the Sea of Faces by the prayers of a single person on Earth?

Can they learn to lust after the light of God, thereby transmuting their attachment, and move on?

In your "Life After Death" reading[1] your descriptions of individual entities were very helpful. Perhaps you could give us similar histories on several entities as they died, entered the Sea of Faces, had experiences, and eventually moved on. In doing so, you could answer the questions above. Please include any and all information that might be helpful or interesting to us.

Thank you, Al and Lama Sing, for your continued work with us in the Earth.

LAMA SING COMMENTARY

Yes, we have the Channel then and, as well, those references which apply to the questions as presented just above.

OPENING COMMENTS

As we come together with you, dear friends, to offer commentary regarding this topic, we should note here clearly that many who have gone before have offered considerable commentary and perspective on this topic. Yet, we would state here, clearly, that this is one of the most significant works that we shall do together with you for the entire tenure of our service with this Channel.

Our reason for stating this to you with no small degree of emphasis is that by understanding the nature and interaction

---

[1] "Life After Death" — This reading is included in Volume I of this series: How to Prepare for the Journey: Death, Dying, and Beyond.

of this topic, in other words, the entities and the realms of consciousness which are involved in same, one can clearly, while yet in the Earth, see the value, the wonderful opportunity, that being in the Earth presents to you all in terms of the "after-life," as it's called, which is the *true* life, the eternal life, *and the potential that that shall bear for you*. So it is our prayer, here, that we are ever worthy and guided in this work, to offer you the highest and best in God's name.

DESCRIPTION

The Sea of Faces, as described by the Channel at the onset above, is in essence perceived by some who pass through it as, literally, a wall of faces; and as they move through this *sea of faces*, they note that there is a vastness to their continuity, as though they may, indeed, be one behind the other ad infinitum.

The Tunnel Is a Curiosity from the "Outside"

It is worthy of note here to state that from their side of the tunnel of light – which is the pathway one creates by their intent in meditation and prayer to move to realms of greater consciousness, to move into states of oneness with God at varying degree or level according to the willingness of the seeker to accept – it is this tunnel of light, then, that is a point of what could be called curiosity, and (to a degree) opportunity, for those who perceive it from the other side, the outside.

This tunnel of light is not seen in the same way as you would see it while passing within it. As you are within the tunnel of light, you are within God's Law and His light and, as that passes through realms which are adjacent to the Earth, to its destination, the Law provides that it does not interfere with the lesser realms, such as those which are categorically defined as "the Sea of Faces." But it is, to many there, visible, detectable, and a point of curiosity and temptation of all sorts.

We believe we shall get into those areas of defining what tempts them and why, in the commentary just ahead and in what we believe shall be, with little doubt, additional such works as will be requested on this topic.

Approaching the Portal

So it is that the Sea of Faces is not just one finite realm but actually a composite of realms. It would be difficult to assign a numerical value to those because they are in a constant state of movement and change; and what we would give in this moment would, several Earth minutes later, be entirely different. It is literally like a sea: constantly moving and changing.

When an entity approaches the portal of departure from the Earth, which you call death, the condition of their spirit, mind, heart, and some degrees of their physical body, have much to do with what happens next.

In this we have, in past, commented; and followed a beautiful soul, whom we called Peter[2] (who, incidentally, is about to work in these realms). But our point in commenting about that here is to point out that growth is always possible, and the opportunity for any entity who is willing (what that means is open and receptive) can be given help at any point, anywhere, any time, according to their willingness.

Therein lies a key of sorts to the movement of souls who are found in the Sea of Faces.

Let us use an example, then, as was suggested in the commentary and questions above. While there is some light-heartedness and a bit of humor intended here in several of the choices, note that these are valid examples, nonetheless.

---

[2] Peter - In 1991, the path Al uses as he's leaving finiteness for his channeled readings crossed with that of a man who was leaving his body through the process we call death. That process and the saga that followed was recorded in what came to be called The Peter Project readings. Those involved in the Peter Project followed Peter through his incredible journey for more than ten years. Easing the fear of dying, giving new hope for life after death, the book, IN REALMS BEYOND is a compilation of the first eighteen months, with future books in the works. A movie and TV series soon to be released is based on this incredible story.

EARTHBOUND EXAMPLE #1:

One Who Lived a Life of Goodness

But Became Trapped in the Sea of Faces

Let us move back in time to what is called the Early West in the North American continent. Here we have an entity who is vigorous in his desire to bring anyone, everyone, unto his flock in God's name... a frontier preacher, if you will. (You have a colloquial term: "a Bible-thumping, fire-and-brimstone preacher," lovingly given. Footnote here...[3]) So, we find this vigorous proponent of the Word of God (or *perpetuator* of the Word of God) at the point of death. Now, there are some serious thoughts going on in this entity's consciousness, for he is asking himself, of all of these things in these many years that he has said to others, how many of them are truly believed in his own heart?

It is at that level of struggle that the "cord" is broken; the life force leaves the physical body and departs from the Earth, upon which it is immediately met by souls of light: guides, perhaps others who are well-intended, if this preacher can stop his inner struggle long enough to perceive them. In other words, long enough to realize that the physical body has been left behind, just so much so as a leaf falling from a tree in its season, see; if he can stop his fretting, his anger with himself, his sadness, his remorse, all sorts of things taking place here... all of which he summates to an inner reflection, which causes a sort of paradoxical situation for this *man of God* (as he might be called), who isn't even looking for God now that he is on a journey which could well take him to realms of consciousness of profound beauty and light.

So it is that, as much as those who are about him are

---

[3] Footnote here – "None of our commentary is judgmental; all souls are equal in our sight, and loved, regardless of whatsoever might be their lot in life or their choice in the moment. See?" -Lama Sing

5

prepared to offer him, are prepared to give to him, unlimited love, unlimited healing grace—*from God*—the entity sees this not. You could say that, instead of moving swiftly at a rate which is incalculable by Earth standards (for there is no reference to time and space, only consciousness, see) instead, the entity drifts slowly. Some entities could be bound to the Earth. Some entities could, in essence... Understand we are giving this for perspective, moreso than the absolute literal, as it occurs. By that, we mean some of the entities who hover around the Earth aren't necessarily (in terms of measurement of the Earth) ten feet, fifty feet, forty meters, twelve leagues, or whatever. It is in *consciousness* that they are in close proximity to the Earth, but still they *are* in close proximity to the Earth because consciousness still is, and has finiteness and definition, and therefore, gravitates to an association with other finiteness.

To translate that a little better here, it's sort of like particle bands: the heavier ones are at the bottom, then the next lighter, and the next lighter, and so on and so forth. So, levels of consciousness which are close in approximation to the Earth could be considered in a parallel to that. We hope that helps. If not, do inquire further.

So, here we have this preacher. Nothing's changed. He thinks of himself just as he was moments ago before death of the body, and he is in this dialogue with himself and moving... We could say (for reference) drifting upwards, slowly. He is not staying upon the Earth, as some (quote) "Earthbound" souls do (end quote) but moving beyond it. He has recognized death to a degree but not fully, see? After a time, he may reach a realm of limited consciousness, whereupon what happens?

You can anticipate, perhaps, based on laws of the Earth (which are, many of them indeed, Universal Laws... God's Laws): Like attracts, in the sense that his thought is going to be responded to by others of like mind. Those others are in what's called the Sea of Faces. As he gradually becomes aware of the fact that there are energies like his own... And it doesn't happen just like that, for it's more subtle than this, indeed, almost charming, alluring. Because he's focused in a certain thought-form, a certain attitude of mind and heart and spirit, he'll notice more swiftly that which is similar because of its familiarity. Follow that? (We are teaching here, in the event that you question why we are asking, and we are also asking for you to think about it.)

So now, he pauses in his journey (which was a sort of meandering one, at best anyway) and here he is at a level of consciousness which rather closely approximates his own as it was just moments before and after the death of his physical body. Feeling this as you would feel a sense of fellowship (whether that be good or bad, see) he begins to open himself. Simultaneously with this, those who are with him attempting to guide him towards the Light also attempt to awaken him to their presence. But remember, these are Light workers, messengers from God, Children of God, often those of the Angelic Host; they will always honor the Law and honor the *primal* Law (or one of the primary Laws): the right of Free Will. Whether in body or not, the Law is perfect, and the workers work within that perfection or, quite simply, they are not workers of the light. See?

If this preacher can open himself to greater potential than his own focused level of consciousness, then the Angelic Host or guides may be able to help him immediately or rather swiftly. If he does not, and his concern or despair or anguish or doubt or fear or whatever it might be causes him to become dependent upon what he senses around him, then he'll likely become an inhabitant of the Sea of Faces at that level, that strata of expression.

What can take place after that is lengthy, and we believe your structure here (according to your questions and instructions) is to not dwell too heavily on that in this meeting but to give the examples as are the questions above, and that we shall attempt to do as best as possible. To briefly comment further, the preacher could remain here, actually, indefinitely... and we do mean indefinitely. There are entities who are in the Sea of Faces from Atlantean times, some of these over two hundred thousand Earth years ago; there are some here, leaders from the

7

great wars of the Earth, still trying to gather forces, still trying to attack what they consider to be enemies; and so on and so forth.

So, here's this preacher and now he has some associates, some colleagues. What will they do? They'll do about the same as they did in the Earth; they'll try to find entities to convert, to preach to. All the while, they'll be questioning within themselves. Of course, they will only find others who are in harmonious vibration with their own level of consciousness, their own thought, the degree to which they are open or not open. As you can see from that, perhaps, the potential for boredom is profound (given with a note of loving humor), which is fortunate, perhaps, in the sense that there would be a greater number than there are in this *Preachers' Realm* (if you will) if it weren't for that.

Now we should add here, because it shall be a question: Can these entities in what we have called the Sea of Faces harm you as you pass through it? Are these entities and their intentions to be feared?

Well, we would answer that in this way: they cannot harm you physically, any more than they can harm each other. Can they harm you spiritually? No, not really, unless you wish to join them. They can feed that desire or that limitation if you accept it. And they will––if they sense that you are of their lot, of their intent, of their (you would call it in the Earth plane) mind-set or intent that will be, to them, an invitation––try to lure you into their realm because of a simple perhaps obvious point, that... [pause] Very well... We are told here is a good colloquial term from the Earth: "misery loves company" (given with a note of loving humor). But it is the Law, which is *Like Attracts,* at least in this type of nomenclature and conditional event.

So the preacher will remain here so long as he wishes. And the guides will remain with him, perhaps not always the same entities (meaning the guides), but generally speaking there will be one or two who are associated primarily with the entity. If the tenure is lengthy and the guides have other works as well,

8

they may come and go, but there will always be at least one, ready constantly to answer if the preacher is ready. See? What do we mean by ready? Well, you would think this man of God, as he called himself when he was in the Earth plane, would always be ready. Which brings us full circle back to our comments above...

Your thoughts, your attitudes, those things which thou thinketh and believe and hold in your heart... they *are* you. Spirit is the pattern, mind is the builder, and the physical is the result; this has been given through Edgar[4] oft times and elsewhere to be sure. Let's expand on that just a bit.

Not only is the physical the result but, through habit, through conditioning, and through the evolution of familiarity (if not fondness) with a certain way of thinking and acting, so do you *become* this in your mental body, in your emotional being and body. And while your spirit is ever, at its highest level of expression, one with God, this aspect of your being is limited by the attitude, the thought.

What you believe – *what thou thinketh in thine heart* – so art thou.

See? It is inescapable. It can be masked; it can be obscured from the vision, for the greater part at least, from others in the Earth (some might see it... those who have the more complete sight will certainly see it), and so on and so forth. An entity can go through their life seemingly, to the general public, one thing, and inwardly be something else; variations here, and all kinds of gradients are possible. (Again, this we do not judge, but merely observe.) So that the thinking in the heart and in the spirit, and whatsoever other facet of self that is not specifically physical or finite, could be included here as well... the psyche, the over-soul, many different terms.

These are usually seen in the spiritual body or energy field of an entity in the Earth; they are felt by those of you who

---

[4] Edgar - Edgar Cayce, a spiritual philosopher and holistic healing pioneer, considered the best-documented psychic/trance channel of the twentieth century.

feel these things while you are in the Earth. In these realms, we see this as the spiritual cloak, as we call it (which is not the physical form but the essence of the entity), and the cloak, if you will, is distorted by these thought-forms, these thought essences, which we categorically define here to help those who are learning to become workers to those in the Earth who are so limited... the *School of Guides* or such, if you will call it that.

EARTHBOUND EXAMPLE #2

One Who Lived a Life of Violence

But Was Free to Transcend

Let's take another individual. This is an entity who has lived in a very intense area of the Earth. There are many entities, in terms of population density, in a very small, relatively speaking, geographical area. There is fierce competition for practically everything—shelter, food, pleasure, all that sort—and there is a continual struggle for many of these entities to dominate and to avoid being dominated.

Here we have an entity who has learned to use his physical body to considerable skill, so that most here in the neighborhood either fear the entity or know better than to attempt to dominate, for they usually would come out worse for their intent. So the entity has lived what you would call by Earth standards a very violent, physical life. A time comes where what you call an accident occurs, and he is lying in the street with many onlookers gathered about him in the process of departure from the Earth, which you call death. As he is lying here, semiconscious, looking up at all these faces looking down at him, all he can think of is, "Oh, my God! Oh, my God!"

In that moment, he is surrounded with light. In the passage of his spirit from his body, he is lifted up in a beautiful tunnel of light, with entities of light embracing him to either side, and he realizes instantly that he is different. The pain is

10

gone. He looks at himself and the other entities, who are radiating naught but love to him, and yet he is grasped firmly on either side by the entities of light, who are guiding him, so to say. This is an action to which he had developed a natural reaction, inwardly, of resistance while he was in the consciousness of the Earth.

Without a thought, he wrenches free from them. They know his thought, and they smile and attempt to communicate to him. In that moment, he flashes back to what could be called an automatic reaction, and he begins to flail about at the entities of light. This goes on for a time (and the entities, as you would surmise, are unaffected by his flurry of quite impressive blows) until he finally wearies of, grows bored by, this, for nothing is happening, no outcome.

So, he now pauses and looks about and speaks to one of the guides with him (who is still smiling) asking, "Who are you? What is this? And am I dead?" They explain each question with an appropriate answer, including, "Yes, your body is dead." To which he answers, "Oh, my God!" and the journey resumes.

Now, how can that simple statement by this adept pugilist of the Earth be an affirmation enabling him to move on? Well, let's look at his life just briefly.

Certainly, he developed impressive physical skills and was feared for them; but he did not seek to use these to dominate others, only to protect himself, to preserve his life and those he loved and who were his. Therefore, he was not seeking dominance, but only his right of endurance and survival and, seeking through this, the only way he knew to preserve his right of free will. In the life in general, he was and is a good man. He cared for those and honored those who had given him life. He helped others; even though not to excess, he did so.

We could continue on here and talk about his rather raucous times on the town with his colleagues, where a bit too much fermented beverage and perhaps other activities that our preacher from the west would have surely condemned him for.

Yet, this man is free from limitation which binds him to lesser realms, and the preacher is trapped. This man, the pugilist, the boxer, is moving on. He is opening himself, and he is excited and joyful. He is apologizing to the guides for his aggressiveness, and they simply smile and assure him they completely understand. And he's excitedly asking, "Will I see Emma? And Walt? What about Aunt Bess?" and they assure him that, in just a moment, these and more will greet him. All the while, what are they doing? They are passing through the Sea of Faces, and all of those faces along the way who would love to increase their number, have no effect upon him. Even a realm wherein all of the entities are in combat constantly, which he was so skilled at, has no appeal to him. The reason for that, obviously, is that his skills were developed out of need, not out of a desire to inflict his will on others.

The light of his spirit is seen in his cloak. Look you here, and you'll see... There isn't darkness. It's fading, and there is light! Yes, there are colors (thoughts) of emotions. Perhaps he shan't go to a realm of great freedom, of, comparatively speaking, considerable acceptance of his spiritual being, but he'll certainly go to those where he'll be nurtured, loved. And he'll be able to learn to receive more knowledge and more awareness, and preparation, should it be advisable and he seeks it, to return to the Earth again. Or, in this case... we should judge by this brilliance in the consistency of the light of his spirit or cloak here... (And we are showing others here...) See? The light is constant, and the colors which are upon that light are not deeply imbedded but more to the surface, so to say.

He will go on, well beyond where he is destined to go in this moment, and we believe he will do that quite rapidly and probably take others with him, or they with them. We are told that there are certain of his grouping (his soul grouping, some of whom were family units in the Earth plane) who have been waiting, not as a burden or a debt but because it is their joy to wait. So this is a life pattern, a life event, which is cause for rejoicing. See?

EARTHBOUND EXAMPLE #3

One Who Could Not Forgive Self

Let us turn to the Earth again, to one more lifetime, which we think will be of some contrast here.

Note that we could give, literally, an unending array of examples which would have an equal number of dispositions or results, for the uniqueness of each soul creates a near infinite array of potential; though, fortunately, that doesn't turn out to be the case because so many entities who cross over the Veil are not deeply imbedded in profound limitations of thought or desire. So these reduce, to a degree, the number of realms and dimensions and such for expression of the needed growth. See? For the Preachers' Realm, as we called it, is an expression of opportunity for all the souls or entities therein, and it exists because of them. It is, collectively, their creation. It has borderlands, if you will consider that an appropriate term, beneath and above, using a linear measure for clarity here, and it is in those borderlands and the sojourns into and out of them that great opportunity for progress can be found. But here again, that begins to digress a bit from the main of the topic, and so we'll return here to our third candidate.

Here we have a woman in Europe about four hundred Earth years previous to your current time in the Earth. In this time period, there is great difficulty, hardship. A vast chasm exists between those who have and those who have not, and so, being born of female body and rather pleasurable for the sight, this woman uses her body to make her way through life, and does so quite well. Becoming the favorite of a certain entity of stature and wealth, she is lifted up from what could have been a very lowly position and placed into special quarters, given special garments, and all that sort. Not an unfamiliar story in the Earth in your present time.

This entity's life moves, then, from poverty and tragedy and abuse and many other things to one of considerable standing, for it is in fashion here for entities of stature to have those consorts whom they keep and it is almost equally of stature to be such a consort. (There are both male and female here. That should be noted, too. We aren't singling the one or the other, but only choosing this entity because she has permitted it... volunteered, if you will, and we'll tell you why just ahead.)

A number of years transpire. The life is good, and she and her friend do share a great deal of wonderful and meaningful times. There is genuine caring between them, even though he has another family elsewhere.

They know that this, in the eyes of their religious belief, is not correct, and they believe, both of them, inwardly, that at some point they must pay for this or be punished. (Neither of these entities have what we would call a very close working relationship with God, given with a note of loving humor. It's more in passing, see?)

The woman has become impregnated, and the birth is troubled. The woman is about to birth the child but shall die in the process. Her friend is at the bedside. His love for her is self-evident, as is hers for he.

She keeps saying to him, "Forgive me," and he says back, "It is I who beg you for forgiveness." She then, of course, states, "You have given me a life, one with such beauty and joy as I would never have known without you and your love." And he responds equally. The child is born. She holds it, and he kisses both and takes the child, and the woman falls into coma.

He can hear her praying and speaking his name, and promising before God that her love shall endure. Simultaneously with this, she is grieving at the wrong she has done to another woman and family.

There is a subtle pop, and she is free of her body. She is weeping, for there are entities whose beauty and radiance are surrounding her. She says to them, with force, "Have I... Am I... dead? Is this the... end?"

One sweet soul comes forward and states, "It is the end of one journey, and the beginning of another. Come. Come with

14

us. Come to the light."

In agony for the affirmation of her sin against another in the Earth and against God, she speaks to them loud and vigorously, "Be gone! I cannot face God. I am filled with sin," and she turns away. She wanders, not unlike the preacher, lamenting and weeping. As she does so, her movement takes her to somewhere, she knows not where. She cannot see the beings of light anymore even though they are yet with her, near at hand, for her own sin—or *belief in* it—has clouded her sight.

Then, she hears cries, cries that echo her own, and she is drawn towards them inexplicably. It is within this realm wherein there are the cries of the lost filling it, grieving for their sin, and so on, and such as this.

This beautiful soul remains here for a time, grieving, and holding others who are grieving as they embrace one another, sobbing on each others' shoulders, describing their sins, their travesties against God, to one another, and then clasping each other, two by two or in groups, sobbing, crying out.

In one of these moments where there was a pause, where she listened to another explain her guilt, her sin, in that moment, she thought of the child she had brought to the Earth, and she thought of the one she loved so dearly. In that moment, she was filled with a light of prayer from the Earth, for in that moment in the Earth, at the bedside of a young lad, a mere eight or nine Earth years in tenure, and kneeling beside him, his father, she heard them pray in her name. See? In this moment this beautiful soul claimed that prayer, and she also claimed the truth of the love which was so pure that she willingly would give her life for either of these entities or both.

We have here in this gathering, standing before us, this same entity, who is learning and sharing along with the others here. We tell you that her beauty is usurped by none in this gathering. Soon, she shall be a guide, a being of light, to another in the Earth. She has chosen to work with those who bear in their heart shadows of darkness, which they impose upon themselves in the belief that they have sinned and are not worthy.

15

She has asked us to tell you, through this work, that she is here to attest that it is true: that God's love has no limit; there is naught in the Earth that God has not already forgiven.

Do what you must to open your heart and to feel free of guilt and sin and, certainly, take action. Do words and deeds of kindness that will enable you to affirm that you are free of this while you are yet in the Earth. If you cannot do this, remember these words when you do pass through the veil of separateness between the Earth and the beyond, that in a time thereafter, should you be limited, you might remember them and remember her story; that you, too, can open and receive the prayers of the Earth, which we and others like us – and many in the Earth, as well, who are growing in number – offer prayer constantly, to help free those who are limited... those who are in the Sea of Faces.

There is much more here, in terms of commentary, and there is much more in terms of what we would call experiences of others which could be shared and we believe shall be in future. But the purity and beauty of this one which we have saved until the last is the thought, the light in your heart, with which we desire to leave you.

CLOSING COMMENTS

We shall turn now to comments which are given from those who walk at the side of the Master, the Christ. They would have us recount to you that, as you journey through the Earth in life and in consciousness, be ever mindful that it is not what you do and say insofar as what shall gain ye in the kingdoms of our Father which lie beyond. It is not the accomplishment of what some call the works of construct or contribution, though these are good. It is not the gift of the material or the financial or such, alone, that gives thee gain in that which is beyond, and we could continue here with examples in that same vein, but we believe and know that it is clear.

So, if it is not these alone, in and of themselves, that make the gain in the kingdoms of our Father, then, what does?

16

It is, dear friends, the intent and spirit with which thou doeth all things, whether they be great or small, that brings to thy path the greater light.

It is, as it has been given in past, truly, upon the arms of those that thou hast helped that ye shall be led into the kingdoms of our Father.

It shall be through the rejoicing and light of those who have been recipients of your loving prayer whose joy and light shall greet thee as you pass through the veil.

It is the small act of kindness that shall endow you with a cloak of light when you leave behind the cloak of flesh and finiteness of the Earth.

Measure yourself and your life according to the ideal within and ever look to this ideal, often, to see, "Is it truly the highest and best that I can perceive? And are the steps along the way—the goals, and the purposes by which I do what I do—in the image of that ideal?"

Lastly, we would offer to you these simple things… and they are truths, dear friends…

There is one unto whom we ask you in humbleness to give your love without limitation. There is one in the Earth we would ask you to forgive without any reservation. There is one whom we would encourage you to support and nurture and to do all good things unto….

…and that is self.

For it is that same self which is the vessel unto which shall bear all other things to those whom you shall meet in life. Within you is the cup, which can and does hold the very spirit of God, that which is present to fulfill the spiritual need or thirst of others.

A lamp has its light within and, as such, casts it all around. It would be well if you would do likewise. For if you honor self, then you have honored God, and you will surely, thereafter, honor others. See?

We are through here for the present, asking that the

grace and blessings of our Father ever be claimed as that lamp to light your way. Fare thee well then for the present, dear friends. Om Shanti.

READING 2: DARK REALMS

AL MINER/CHANNEL: This is March 27, 1998. This is a request for a topical research reading, and the title is The Sea of Faces, Part II.

I'll read the comments and questions that I have received for this second reading in this series. They write:

QUESTIONS

Lama Sing, thank you for your first reading on the Sea of Faces. This is a second topic reading, and we are going to submit some more questions. We would welcome more case studies as your answers to these questions.

The Channel recently had an experience of hearing voices, probably from the Sea of Faces? Why did this happen? Is it closer to the Earth now than it was in past?

The Sea of Faces seems to be different from other realms. It seems "sticky", a place where entities get stuck and, therefore, very undesirable. What makes the Sea of Faces different from other realms?

If we have an addiction and have attracted entities from the Sea of Faces, do we usually attract the same entities, like negative guides who are attuned to our vibrations? Or are they always changing? If we suddenly pray for them, does that help them?

For years you have prayed for those "for whom there are none in joyous prayer." Is this for those in the Sea of Faces?

It seems easier to pray for people when we have a name to focus on. How should we pray for individuals in the Sea of Faces? What should our spiritual work consist of?

Please give more examples of how entities "escape" from this realm.

(And this addendum, this additional question, was telephoned in:)

Lama Sing, what is the role of laughter in keeping us from entering the Sea of Faces, or getting stuck in the Sea of Faces, or helping entities get out of the Sea of Faces?

Please include any and all information that might be helpful or interesting to us.

Thank you, Al and Lama Sing.

I would like to add here that my transcriber and I have had a number of discussions about this topic. If you would like to offer us any comment on what we've discussed, or in general, that too would be welcomed.

LAMA SING COMMENTARY

We would encourage that the first question regarding the Channel's experience stand alone, in that this will be of significance, and differently so than the general topic which is now before us. We will suggest, as well, that this be a work which is done according to guidances which shall be given directly to the Channel in terms of the specifics of the environ and timing and such. We thank thee.

To answer in the general sense the first question, those criterion or circumstances or environmental aspects are different in the present, and this has facilitated the experience which he related and unto which question number one is directed. See?

OPENING COMMENTS

The Sea of Faces is different than other, as called, realms. In the general sense, it could be thought that the Sea of Faces is indeed many realms, rather than one. This brings us to the point of establishing a common reference point between us as to the definition of the word or term "realm".

As we have previously given (to briefly recapitulate here) you could, for sake of reference, see the realm structure as ranging from one to seven, and in essence actually having a realm above and below those seven primary realms, generally speaking.

20

Those seven major realms each are constructed of sub-realms, of which, in the general sense, we could again apply the same numerical structure of one to seven or, if you prefer, nine... that latter number, including the one foundational above and below the other seven. See? (We trust this is not confusing.) Then you could take, certainly, each sub-realm and define that further, and in fact you could actually do this ad infinitum so to say, within reason. So that would be one reference point: seven major realms of expression, consciousness, and experience unto which souls move (using linear reference for sake of understanding) ever upward as their degree of spiritual acceptance grows. See?

If an entity, conversely, falls into categorically what is called the Sea of Faces, then the normal reference points (in terms of linear numeric value) do not have such a clear, concise application and value as reference points.

The Nature of the Sea of Faces

Now comes perhaps the difficult part for you to comprehend, and for us to explain to you. It is our prayer that we shall do well for you.

Consciousness does not conform to linear movement, in other words, straight-line movement. Neither does consciousness confine itself to the implied dimensional references that are supposed in linear reference or movement. So we could literally move, in essence, at right angles or any variation upon same from the straight, linear movement. In other words, if you draw a straight line upwards, the Sea of Faces can have movement (as could other entities, as well, to be sure), but those who move about in the Sea of Faces do so at angles, so to say, to normal movement. They can move vertically or linearly. But remember, consciousness must match the realm of expression.

So, if an entity moves from Earth through the portal called death and they are so limited or so bound to the Earth in one manner or another as to be in the Sea of Faces, could it follow then, logically, that they would move to a higher realm?

See the meaning? They could not sustain consciousness there for any prolonged period of Earth time. See?

So they are in the bardo, the hinterland, the borderland, and many other names... even such as called by some, purgatory. It is different in many respects than those names imply, although, in some instances, descriptively and literally, those names or titles are quite accurate, unfortunately.

If you would now consider movement in consciousness to be more than simply linear, straight-line movement such as you are accustomed to in your measurement of time and distance and all that sort, consider the aspect of dimensions. Consider the aspect of altered states of consciousness, which are beyond the Earth and yet near it, and sometimes within it.

Altered states of consciousness are a part of the Sea of Faces, in the sense that entities can leave behind, so to say, some of their (quote) "normal consciousness" (end quote) and move into a state of consciousness which is their own creation. In other words, they dwell in a consciousness of their own limitation (that is, for all practical purposes to the participant who is in same, a realm), but the entity is not complete in the literal sense.

They are only a portion or particle of their total being, just so as entities who are alive and conscious in the Earth do not, in the normal sense, constantly sustain the fullness of their spiritual awareness... save those such as the Master, Buddha, Krishna, and others, many of them, who have attained that state of enlightenment.

So, while this might seem at the onset to be odd and very unique information, if you dwell upon it, if you meditate and reflect upon it intellectually, we believe that you will rather quickly grasp it; and not only that, but comprehend why it is so. So we gave the reference points for you to construct a visual picture of moving at angles to the straight-line, normal progression of the soul as it grows in spiritual acceptance. Well, this gives you a concept of the nature of the Sea of Faces.

Potential Influence of the Sea of Faces

It could co-exist with other expressions of consciousness and neither would be knowledgeable of the other's presence. Except that, as entities in the alternate dimensions (or realms of consciousness) have the same vibration, the same energies, the same desires, if you will, this makes a connection of sorts.

Which leads us into, does it not, a further discussion on Earthbound souls, and one of your questions: the potential influence those souls can have. Yes, the Sea of Faces is a multi-dimensional realm, which actually lies between realms, in a sense. Moving outwards towards the opposing polarities of a median point, it becomes more and more diffused. Generally speaking, as you move upwards from that median point towards the next major realm or next sub-realm above it, you would find that the influence of the Sea of Faces diminishes. Hence, as entities do move upwards in their spiritual acceptance, their potential for becoming free of the Sea of Faces increases directly proportionate to the decrease of intensity of influence of the Sea of Faces itself.

Very well, we shall continue in this manner to attempt to clarify this even further. You commented in your questions, using the term (quote) "sticky" (end quote). This is very appropriate, in the sense that like attracts in terms of intentions and/or desires, goals, limitations and, generally speaking, thoughts, attitudes, and so on. Of course, it is quite understandable that an entity with an addiction of significant degree might struggle to cling to that source of addiction, even after passing through the veil of separateness through the portal called death in the Earth. And if this is sufficiently intense or the desire sufficiently powerful, it can limit or halt their forward progress into greater spiritual acceptance, and, in a sense, almost tether them to the Earth as a plane of focus and consciousness. Yet, simultaneously, they no longer have a physical body, physical senses, nor the mechanisms through which physical bodies gain gratification through varying desires or whatnot.

Noting here very quickly that these are not perceived as

23

(quote) "bad," see, unless they limit the entity in the manner as those entities in the Sea of Faces are so limited. Then the (quote) "badness" of it is in their lack of joy and the gradual decay of their consciousness, which would otherwise, in the normal sense, rise to its greatest potential of spiritual acceptance.

So, addictions are, as such, like tethering the spirit of the entity to the Earth or to the focal point or source of their addiction. Since they have just departed from the Earth, it is presumed that that would be the Earth itself. As this occurs (immediately after departure from the Earth, of course) an entity with an addiction is going to gravitate to others who have similar energies, vibrations, thought-forms, and the like. And vice-versa, those already in the Sea of Faces will look for comrades... surprisingly, because, even in limited consciousness, they know that the greater is the number in their consciousness (or realm of consciousness), the more permanent and powerful, from their perspective, does it become. They cannot force, they cannot violate Universal Law, but the natural order of progression, the natural rhythm of Universal Law, presents each soul with reference points that are intended to strengthen, intended to enlighten and give knowledge, which can grow into wisdom, and all this sort.

If you look at this from the macrocosmic, arm's-length viewpoint, you will see that even those in the Sea of Faces are doing just that... they will learn, they will grow. The question is how quickly, when, where, and how, as reiterated in your questions.

Idiosyncrasies of the Sea of Faces

What makes, generally speaking, the Sea of Faces different from other realms? Denial.

Think about that... denial. When an entity in the Earth denies their oneness with God, they become limited. When an entity denies themselves the joy of living life with all of the senses as bright and brilliant and receptive as possible, they become limited. When an entity refuses to care for their body, even though they might know that such needs are important, they are denying their bodies. When an entity withholds love and compassion and kindness, generosity, patience, and all the virtuous words and terms and such that you can muster, they are denying them, as well, of self or selves.

Again, remember, the Law Universal is perfect. To deny something that is normal... In other words, it is normal for you to love and be loved; if you deny this to others, you are denying it to yourself. It is curious to many here that this is not understood in the Earth. Yet, we know as we are gathered here that, from the perspective of the Earth, the continuum of thought-form is profoundly powerful, and those who live in the reality of the collective thought-form in the moment find it difficult to escape its dominance. It is ever present, almost omnipotent, as you walk about in physical body in the Earth, is it not? Yet, those who reach beyond that thought-form find truth, experiment with it, discover it to be good, and then live it. These entities do not walk in the thought-form of Earth, alone. They also walk in realms of light and enlightenment simultaneously as they walk about in the Earth. This is a point of importance for future reference.

When you claim the truth of your nature, when you allow yourself to express love with little or no expectancy of return, only for the joy of expressing it, you make certain that this shall be your just return. As you enable yourself to do this, and do it consistently, a portion of your being breaks free of the mass-mind thought-form of Earth and walks in realms of Light.

We know that may be difficult to grasp, but it is true. You become, simultaneous to your physical expression, a being of light. Those who accomplish this through varying means – oft times seemingly a happen-stance or coincidence or accident, nonetheless it happens; some by deliberate, dedicated persistence to their ideal; and others because of soul purposes which were brought with them as they entered into the Earth but the result is the same – their light body is awakened and freed.

This occurs for all entities under certain circumstances, if they allow it and, in some instances, even when they do not intend to do so. One of these is in the dream state, and this is widely known. Another is in meditation. Yet another can occur during prayer, particularly when you set forth to do work in and about the Sea of Faces through your prayer intent.

It is this, in part at least, unto which we give that prayer at the onset of most all of our gatherings with you (or that which you call *readings*). We do this to open the doorway, so to say... to cast aside the blinds, that for those who are willing to receive, the light is offered. We do this for other reasons, which are too complex (and very interactive between our groups and other groupings of light workers, guides, and such) to explain in this setting or sitting and still comply with the questions before us, so we'll leave that as an addendum for future, if you desire that information.

Again, Peter is one of those who is about to begin such works. (Peter being an entity, for those who know him not, who we followed for many Earth years in previous research projects, with a goodly number of beautiful souls who are in the Earth.)

So we should think here that this gives sufficient, for the moment, at least, differentiation about the idiosyncrasies of the Sea of Faces. We grant you, it is only a small look into that, but our prayer is that it gives you somewhat greater insight than you had previously.

HOW THE SEA OF FACES WORKS

To summarize, then, the Sea of Faces is a realm, and yet it is not in the sense of reference to the seven major realms. It is also multi-dimensionally expressed at different angles to the prime line of movement. See?

Like Attracts Like

Like attracts, that is true. If an entity has an addiction, generally speaking, those in the Sea of Faces, or those who are Earthbound who have a similar desire, focus, or need, will be drawn unto that. They won't be drawn to the addict as the individual, but they can be drawn to the weakness or the energy that is the result of that need or weakness on the part of the addict.

So, look at this in this manner... Supposing for a moment that you consider that each entity walks about in the Earth plane surrounded by a sort of spherical orb of energy, vibration, sort of like a cloak that covers the entity completely. That cloak of energy (or aura, if you like that term) is comprised of color, sound, odor, vibrational essences that are multi-dimensional in their expression and manifestation. You can even have something similar to what you would consider taste involved. In other words, easily spanning the breadth of your normal five physical senses and reaching out to involve other (as they could be called from your perspective), senses or stimuli, as well. So, it's akin to some of your scientific experiences, or experiments, in the Earth, conditioned response and all that sort, as with Pavlov (and the others, see... Sigorski and many).

As an entity in the Sea of Faces feels, detects, or perceives something that is at the same vibrational frequency as their primary focus—which would be their addiction or need, see; or could be the inverse of this, the causal effect of that need (there again, another rather broad area of discussion, potentially)—then they will, of course, move towards that. It is like a light in the darkness to them (however, we hasten to add, it is not the Light or God's Light, in that sense). It is the essence of that which they seek, like the odor of fresh baked bread in the Earth. See? Draws you to it, does it not? Like the sound of gentle water caressing the seashore. You gravitate towards that and remember thoughts which are relevant to that. In the Sea of Faces, entities do just that.

So, to answer that portion of your question, you often will attract the same entities because they will have zeroed in on you (given with a note of loving humor). Entities in the Sea of Faces do not have a very broad range of perception. In other words, if they are focused on one specific geographical place in the Earth, they can detect or perceive stimuli from a general

27

geographic area that might only be several miles or perhaps ten to fifteen kilometers in circumference, see… approximate. This varies from entity to entity, but as a general measure. Think about it. They won't know of that, generally speaking, as it occurs in the next geographical state of your country, referring to the North American. Could they? Yes, but they would have to leave, release their focus upon, what, more often than not, is a finite location. Generally, this is often their last place of residency in the Earth (and, of course your logical thinking would probably conclude that anyway). Some entities may *migrate*, to use that term loosely, if they believe that they can find a location where the preponderance of energies might be even greater than that one upon which they are focused, but these are more so the exception than the rule. So, yes, you do generally attract the same entities, but not always or only those entities.

A Concentration of Discarnates

If you live in a highly populated geographical area and you have an addiction, there are lots of different entities to compete for close proximity to you, your addiction affording them stimulus to attempt to relive their own memories. Some entities, as with alcohol, will try to compete with one another, see? In other words, non-physical entities will compete with one another to occupy the same time and space as a drunken entity's physical body, because time and space and dimension intersect, and where the voluntary drunkenness occurs, the greatest stimulation of that as a potential to re-kindle their own memories (the discarnate entity's) of their own experiences of being drunken, tipsy, as called in some countries.

So, where the vibrations or the energies or the thought-forms, the emotions – all are true – are the most concentrated or intense, you will, likewise, find the greatest concentration of discarnate entities also gathered. They can contribute a subtle energy to the physical realm to limited degree, and the moreso is the length of their tenure in the Sea of Faces, the more adept they become at doing this and at their attempts to manipulate entities in the Earth. They can't literally do this, but they can make this a constant thought around those who are known to have weakness or susceptibility to those thoughts. They can't make the addict do that thing to which they are addicted, but they can create an atmosphere that continually reminds them, heightens the desire, like the odor of the fresh baked bread makes you want to eat some (for most, anyway).

Guides for Those in the Sea of Faces

There are perhaps, colloquially (as you called it) negative guides, although that raises quite a fervor here (given with a note of loving humor). The guiding of such entities from the Sea of Faces wouldn't take you anywhere near the potential joy and love of God's light but 'round and 'round in a circle, see, a sticky one at that. No, they are not always changing, but they can and do change.

Some [discarnates in the Sea of Faces] have more power than others, and they become dominant and bump the others from positions of closest proximity to the source of their need or desire.

WAYS TO HELP

Yes, of course, if you suddenly pray for them, that's like shining a bright light in their eyes, and they will back off as far as they need to, equivalent or proportionate to the power and intent or dedication or… You coined an acronym in past: PPUs – Prayer Power Units; if you have lots of those, then they'll back a long way off and might not even come back. See? Prayer is a light.

It is always good to begin a work being done in the Earth plane with an affirmation, with a prayer. If for no other reason than that we've just given above, wouldn't you think it to be so?

We cannot state in the literal sense that that helps them, but it certainly helps you, particularly if you have an addiction. You are then better enabled to deal with it yourself without the subtleties of their temptations being constantly waved in front of you. So, the moreso they cannot satiate their needs from those who are in the Earth, the moreso must they face it themselves. To that degree, then, you are helping with your spontaneous prayer.

It does awaken them for a few brief moments, after which they either allow themselves to be purified or they move back. Of course, there are all varying numbers of gradients and degrees between the two extremes, see, the one being acceptance, and the other protection and immediate departure to a safe place where they can nurture their desire.

Those for Whom There Are None in Joyful Prayer

It is true that we have prayed for those who have none in joyful prayer on their behalf. Not all of those souls who lack joyful prayer are in the Sea of Faces, however; unless, of course, you are willing to expand the Sea of Faces to include entities who are in physical body. What do you think about doing this? Would it be appropriate? Do you think such a consideration has validity? In other words, would you consider, from the definitions and knowledge that you have to this point about entities in the Sea of Faces, that there could be considered entities who are in physical body – incarnate rather than discarnate, see – who are actually in the Sea of Faces? We'll just leave this at that point for you, all of you, to consider and perhaps to discuss with your groups, if you are blessed to have them (study groups, that is).

Well, in short, for now, yes, it is for those who are in the Sea of Faces, for they always come to movement along the lines of light. They know that they can approach it at close proximity… it being a line of light, or a tunnel of light, or whatsoever you would like to call same. They can do so without any threat to them and the maintenance of their limitation. In other words, it will be their choice. They can have, almost literally, their nose against the light and still sustain the uniqueness of their individuality at its current point of expression. That is how, in our earlier meeting with you regarding the Sea of Faces, that phrase became coined; that just on the other side of the Tunnel of Light as you move through it you might perceive what seems to be an endless wall of faces: peering, looking, beckoning, and all that sort. But they cannot enter in. Even if they could, they would not, for the most part. (There are exceptions here, too, but generally, the same tunnel that preserves you preserves them... perfect, just according to the Law Universal or God's Universal Law.)

The Power of Prayer

When we offer our opening prayer for those who have none in joyful prayer on their behalf, we are offering it simultaneously into all of existence, not just the Sea of Faces. We can do this because it is in accordance with the *Law of Love*, which simply means that we can make an offering of love simultaneously everywhere at once, and those who are seeking it will find it given to them. If they are in the lesser realms of light, they can follow that prayer to us – or others who are of the Angelic Host, or guides or such – and the way will be made passable for them, and a way of light will be opened unto them.

This is but one aspect of the power of prayer. When you unite it with knowledge of God's Law, you become a worker in the light in the truest sense of that term.

If you go to the top of a great mountain and shout down into a canyon, you may hear an echo, a reverberation that seems to repeat itself again and again and again. But even in the most profoundly splendid of these geographic locations, in short order you can no longer hear what you have shouted. In the eternal sense, when you pray it is like standing upon a mountain top, shouting out into space and time with words of loving light *that never stop.* Prayer is the eternal expression of loving light, *if* the intent is of that nature. That is the method and the application which we use in our opening and closing prayer.

In Prayer, The Value of Having a Name

It is easier to pray for someone when you have a name, for the name is the entity's *code*: it is their resonance, it is their identity, it is their tonal vibration for that consciousness. In oth-

31

er words, if it is a lifetime consciousness, it's like dialing their spiritual telephone number. If they are in the Sea of Faces, then it is the same; it is like sending a focused beam of prayer directly to the intended destination, rather than broadcasting it generally and hoping that entity is tuned to that broadcast. (So you are precisely correct, see? Just supporting you in that.)

Wherever possible, if you can have the name and location and whatnot of the entity who is in need of prayer, they'll receive it more fully, more immediately, and with the greater completeness of your intent, your loving intent, than they would without it. In ninety percent of the cases, this would be true, or greater, see? (We're told ninety-two would be the most accurate. Within the remaining eight percent, other variations apply.) If you can find an entity in the Sea of Faces and be cognizant of them, you create a line of light. If you meditate upon that, you can create *an address,* which is the same as a name or vibratory identifier that will activate that line of light between you that will function similarly to knowing their name.

Conversely, you can ask in meditation for the names of those who most need your prayers in this moment and listen... have faith... believe... and pray for the names which you are given. The greater is your faith and dedication, the greater shall your service become; and very quickly you will find yourself surrounded by beautiful entities of light seeking your prayers for those whom they serve as guides or as angelic light forces. Prayers from those in the Earth plane are very powerful, because your free will is total there, and your Universal Consciousness is in a position that makes this extremely powerful and important. Plus, Universal Law is in action here. The Sea of Faces is at your realm of expression moreso than any other, see, so you have the right to do works therein.

We would always encourage you to pray: state an affirmation, and then meditate and ask what your spiritual work should consist of at any given point, in any given individual work session (if we might call it such). But to answer the question and offer general guidance, we suggest you do as we just gave—meditate after prayer and affirmation, and listen. If you don't get a name, you'll get a feeling, an impression, some form of identifier, some connective line of what we call light, which may be different for you in your perception or in your nomenclature but the result would be the same.

It's like creating a pathway between you. If you affirm that and use it and follow it, good works can be accomplished. If the recipient is willing, which they probably are or you wouldn't know of them, you could be God's instrument which frees them, which makes the way passable for them to move on. Your love, your prayer, given open-handedly so to say, has wondrous potential. Those who are open, even subtly, can be helped greatly.

The Power of Laughter

You spoke of laughter, and we know that you have some concept of this; but in honor to your questions, we offer the following.

What is laughter, if not the expression of a Child of God who has, in that moment, claimed their heritage? Laughter is the ability to see that which was in the moment prior to same, significant, permanent, in many ways, finitely restricting and, through the medium of laughter, immediately transform this into the passing moment, into a more appropriate position in the psyche, in the consciousness, in the reality, which is eternal.

Humor is the gift of the angels to those who are willing to receive same that is of their own nature. Humor is the expression of love when it has been unfettered, unleashed, or released. Humor creates a pathway of light through which or upon which love and all the other aspects of God's grace can freely move. Do you not feel, when you are in a state of joyful laughter with another or with a group, a unique bond with them, even if but for a fleeting moment? Laughter is light. Laughter is the music of the eternal nature of your soul. It is possible to move anywhere, everywhere, using the vehicle which you call laughter, if it is a joyous laughter expressed with love, with joy, in the completeness of your being. There are, perhaps, qualifiers (or so it would seem) and of course, as you might anticipate, there would be these. But generally, if you know the finiteness of the Law not... in other words, you don't know the specifics of the Law... you aren't responsible for them. Your laughter, then, would be just as powerful as the most learned practitioner.

The paradoxical balance-point to that sort of *free passage* (if you will) wherein, if you don't know the specifics of the Law you aren't in that moment held accountable for them, that does not mean they don't continue to work; but you are preserved and protected, and the intent of your heart prevails. Now, at the paradoxical balance point, if you are intimately aware of the specifics, the minutiae, of that certain Law or aspect of it, you become as the skilled surgeon with fine implements, able to reach in and remove dis-eased tissue... with only the most seemingly subtle effort, a precision work.

When you laugh, you are in your Light body. That should answer your question about the effect of laughter as a preventative from getting into the Sea of Faces and getting stuck there. What happens is, laughter energizes the spiritual cloak around you. Remember that orb we described around you, which is comprised of a collage, a plethora, of energies and an incredible array of interactive complexities in the combination frequency, density, intensity, and so on and so forth? Laughter activates the entirety of this, if it is full, according to that as we just gave, with light.

Imagine, then, someone who has an addiction, who has been (quote) "hanging around you to satiate their desire" (end quote) suddenly gets a blast of Light by way of your laughter. They have two immediate choices: to depart or to participate.

Laughter has a curious quality: it's purifying. It won't take away the addiction, but it goes directly to the cause. Why is that entity addicted? Perhaps they had no laughter in their previous lifetime, and this was their escape.

Laughter creates a gateway of light, and if the entity in the Sea of Faces who is embraced by your laughter so wishes, they can easily pass through that gate and never return, ever again, to the Sea of Faces, unless they consciously choose to and that is highly unlikely. If they do return, undoubtedly it would be as a light worker trying to help others as they, themselves, have been helped.

Laughter is the music of Universal Law. Laughter is the Spirit of God going out to touch Itself. Those who open themselves to laughter are receiving a gift from you just so as any other you might offer them... *any* other! Laughter is the catalyst which can transform darkness into light, which can bring life where it had previously been weakened. Laughter is the balm which heals wounds of the heart and spirit. Think of laughter as the *castor oil pack* for the soul.

If you can get a good round of laughter going, offer a prayer of invitation to any and all who are in close proximity to you or to the Earth to join in, then see what comes from this. We should think it will be noteworthy.

CLOSING COMMENTS

We haven't given the examples that you sought regarding entities escaping from the Sea of Faces, but in a sense you have given your own examples in your questions.

Escaping

The Sea of Faces could be thought of as a sub-realm of the Earth, or sub-realms in the plural sense. It could also be thought of as secondary to other dimensions and such as that. But for the sake of your question, think of what binds entities: that which gives them shelter or which enables them to hide their weakness, their frailty, their inadequacy, their sense of guilt, their need, their desire, their limitation, their thirst. What quenches it?

Look at the Sea of Faces as a place for those who are in denial, as we gave above. Whether they feel they have sinned or their guilt is too great or that God will know their weakness, their frailty, if He but sees them, they wish to hide this. The addict is as much self-condemning and burdened with sadness or having an absence of some quality which would make them complete. If you wish to help them escape, then do as you are doing, and do more of it. Listen for your guidance, and work with it. Speak to that. Know it to be valid. Have faith.

More will be given on this and related issues, and that question regarding the channel above, as you seek it. For the present, we shall conclude.

Fare thee well then for the present, dear friends.

Om Shanti.

READING 3: CRY OF THE LOST

AL MINER/CHANNEL: This is March 30, 1998. This is a request for a topical research reading. According to my guidance and your comments in the previous reading, entitled the *Sea of Faces, Part II,* I am requesting this topical research reading as a continuation of that latter reading. You urged me in that reading to meditate and seek guidance as to when and how to present this request, and I am following that to the best of my ability and awareness. I am going to title this reading Cry of the Lost.

QUESTION

In the Sea of Faces reading, Part II, our first question was, "The Channel recently had an experience of hearing voices, probably from the Sea of Faces? Why did this happen? Is it closer to the Earth now than it was in past?" So that was the question that we presented that resulted in your urging to seek this as a separate reading.

NOTES FROM AL'S JOURNAL

I'm going to read from my journal notes of that experience, which happened on January 11, 1998, and I've noted that it was 3:00 a.m. I'm quoting from my journal:

Hearing the Cry

"After a very restless night of trying to fall into sleep, I awoke at about 3:00 a.m. and decided to get a cup of coffee and go out onto the deck. It was a still and mild evening, and the sky was so very clear. The moon was two days from being full. It was beautiful. As I stood there, perhaps with an altered, or less than normal, consciousness from trying to sleep, I heard this strange sound. It was like many voices in the distance. When I shifted my senses to better hear, I was shocked. I could clearly hear wailing, moaning, crying. There were so many voices, it was hard, if not impossible, to focus on just one.

"The sense of despair and/or loneliness was overwhelming. It wrenched my heart and soul. It took my breath away. I was flooded with the emotion of those cries. It so stunned me that I heard myself gasp aloud. I pulled away from it and paced back and forth.

"Perhaps five or more minutes passed, and I finally went back inside. Then, thinking I might have imagined the cry, or that my hearing had deceived me and it was only some 'night sound', I went back out onto the deck.

"At first, there was only stillness, and the beauty of the moonlit sky relaxed me. Then I heard it again. This time, it was louder and clearer. I don't recall how long I listened, but finally I couldn't bear to hear any more. It was pitiful beyond description. I quickly went back inside and sat down and said an affirmation and prayers for those souls. Inside my apartment, I heard nothing."

Sharing the Experience

Then I wrote here: "The notes above at the beginning of this are from that affirmation, prayer, and meditation time." I later (I think it was the next day or two later) spoke to Ken, who prepared and submitted the questions, specifically the one above.

It was very curious to both of us that we immediately went to a topic of conversation that was identical. In other words, he had called to talk about the possibility of doing some readings, some research, on the general topic of the Sea of Faces. So, when I told him of my experience a day or two earlier, well, it was somewhat startling to both of us.

So, Lama Sing, we prayerfully ask that you now explain to us why you felt this should be done as separate work. We are not certain what specific questions to ask. As I re-read from my journal for this recording, I can remember and vividly feel the emotion that I experienced that morning.

LAMA SING COMMENTARY

Yes, we have the Channel then and, as well, those references which apply to the topic as presented just above and those inquiring minds and hearts as are gathered about these works.

OPENING COMMENTS

First, we shall express to you our gratitude for conforming to our request, and we shall attempt herein to comply with the earlier questions and, as well, afford you a better understanding of why our request was given as such.

Reason for the Suggestion

In the experience as described by the Channel (and as, very appropriately, recorded from his journal entry), there can be clearly noted that such an experience does have some power as relates to the emotional aspects of self. In particular, this might well impact someone in the Earth plane consciousness who, having heard same and being *open* while so doing, might be heavily impacted. Therefore, it was our advisement here (and carefully considered) that this work should stand alone, just in the event that recalling those experiences might invoke some residual emotional impact upon this our Channel.

Because of the methodology and the activities which are present during the course of any such work which is done through this, our Channel, a considerable degree of "openness" (perhaps put that in quotes, as well, entity Nancy [the transcriber]) is required, as might be clearly understood in the Earth. There is also the requirement of the setting aside of Self (capital "S") in order that there can be the clearest possible channel or pathway through which the information can be given. In the process of accomplishing that, this (and most all channels of like procedure and work) would relegate themselves in an attitude of affirmation, prayer, and faith, to be, just so, utterly and completely as is within their capability, open.

That openness, then, is our responsibility in the name of the Christ. So as the Channel offers this open-handedly to God, and we as His servants respond in God's name, this becomes ours to protect, to govern, to the best as is our potential to so do, and, according to Universal Law, as we are permitted. These, then, are the considerations as were given us, and as we considered, and therefore requested of you in the Earth. See?

DISCOURSE

Yes, the Sea of Faces as a general collective realm, or place of consciousness so to say, is in closer proximity to the Earth than in past. And this proximity is in a state of continual change, moving closer to the Earth, as it were, or vice-versa. (It is difficult to give you a reference point in terms of which is moving this way or that, but rather simply understand that there is movement.) It is proceeding continually and there is a gradual increase to it as is relevant to the overall activities which are present in the Earth plane at this time. Add to that that this is universal… this movement, see?

So then, not just the Earth, but, in general, all consciousness is afforded the opportunity of change, of growth, or if you prefer the terms, movement, or progress.

2:00 – 4:00 AM

In the circumstances which the Channel described, the awakening at that particular time was fortuitous in the sense that, number one, he was correct in his assumption that, yes, he was in somewhat of an altered state due to the broken sleep pattern he had experienced prior to awakening at 3:00 a.m. This, too, would apply for most entities. We have in past encouraged entities to come together at a meditation time during the period 2:00 to 4:00 a.m. Sleeping for a time and awakening is conducive to receptivity because much of the constant thought patterns of the Earth, often referred to here as mass-mind thought, are at a very low level of function. Secondly, moving from a sleep state to an awakened state in the time frame does make one more receptive or more open than would be the norm. Why is this? If there has been, as we have suggested, a period of three to, let's say, five Earth hours of sleep (or something in that range), then an altered state of consciousness has been attained, no doubt, wherein normal consciousness has been released during that time. This could be thought of as freeing the spirit of self and movement, travel, spiritually, mentally, and/or in what is referred to by some as the astral body.

So coming back to a physically awake state after such affords one greater opportunity than, let's say, one might have at mid-day when meditating for the reasons we have given above. We would quickly add here that this is not to imply that there are not those who can accomplish these states of meditation at any time, for that is certainly true. We are pointing out that the environmental circumstances make this easier, requiring less effort. (We should think this might be understandable from the Earth plane, based upon what we have given; that shall be our prayer here.)

A Realm of Denial

The Sea of Faces – particularly those who have been indwelling there for some considerable (as you measure it in the Earth plane) time – is a place of consciousness, perhaps, moreso than a physical dimension or realm from which intensity of focus is commonplace. This is largely due to denial on the part of the souls therein, denial in the sense of, for varying reasons, being unable to or unwilling to accept their greater spiritual potential and (colloquially given) to *move on.*

The sound and emotion which the Channel perceived and which recoiled him so substantially was and is the thought-forms, the emotions, the feelings, and the position of consciousness of certain groups of souls who are in, currently, that which we call the Sea of Faces.

Others can hear this, not just this Channel. Others can seek it and connect with it and know it, and perhaps there might be some value for others to so do, if for no other reason than to validate for yourselves the immensity of this experience; and to convey, perhaps, by being cognizant of this, the potential for

41

wondrous works that such knowledge of this affords all of you.

In terms of potential benefits, not the least of which here is also that of awakening you to the power, the control, and the potential that you have while yet in the Earth to eliminate the Sea of Faces as a potential destination for you upon your departure from the Earth... or rather, if you prefer, when you *die* (which is a misnomer to be sure, but it is of familiar usage in the Earth, hence we have given it, see?)

The Majority Pass Through

We do not wish to impart an attitude generally of fear in regard to this entire topic; or to suppose, either figuratively or literally, that this is a very, very real danger for all of you, because that is simply not so.

The majority of souls departing from the Earth pass through the Sea of Faces; some slowly, some swiftly, and some almost immediately so as to leave the impression that such a realm or dimension is non-existent. And that is as it should be, according to the awareness of the soul who is traversing these realms.

But the greater one can understand that such realms of expression do exist, and that they have as inhabitants a staggering number of souls, and to understand further that this is a potential of limitation or imposition at the very least for many others who are yet in the Earth, then we should think that this knowledge and the experiences which you can produce from same are well worthy of this small effort.

Not Literally Lost

The *Cry of the Lost* is an appropriate term and/or title for this work. Let's explore briefly here why we might state that. Are these souls literally lost? No, they are not; but, for all practical purposes, from their perspective, they are.

It may seem incredible to you, but because they believe they are lost, they are lost; because they have accepted limitation, they are limited, even when, as a collective group of great number, they might reach a point of almost unbearable sadness, remorse, loneliness, and all that sort, sufficient so as to produce the cry that this, our Channel, heard, and others of you as well.

Why do they not simply release their limitation? Why do they believe they are lost, in the very first place or very first point of their decision? Well, we shall comment on this and other such.

The questions which we just posed may seem, at first listening, to be very difficult to understand. If you are one of those who falls into that grouping, consider these points: You are creations of God, you are *Children of God*. Therefore, as Children of God, within you are the seeds of God's own omnipotence. His power and His Law are within you, just as surely as genetic patterns are within your physical body from your physical and/or biological heritage. So this, then, supports the righteousness of Free Will, does it not? Certainly, according to Universal Law, that is so. Therefore, those who are (colloquially called) Light workers – angels, guides, or servants of the Light and so forth – will always honor the Law Universal, for they know this to be perfect. It is, within their being, a totality and, therefore, the consideration of violating it does not occur to them.

Even in the midst of the Sea of Faces there are such glorious beings of Light, awakened Children of God, if you will, who are continually willing to serve; looking for and, with incredible patience, awaiting a moment wherein one or more souls may open themselves, may release their powerful hold on their own guilt and remorse and unworthiness and accept, for just one moment, a greater blessing. It is their belief that they have wronged God or wronged others, or both, that suppresses their receptivity to the Light; that inhibits their potential to grasp, even conceptually, that this too might be forgiven. See?

Comfort in Company

As they are gathered into groupings, and those groupings into masses, the cry (that, in this instance, the Channel heard) was indeed a cry of lost souls: their cry of sorrow for the

43

wrongs they had committed, for the errors of omission as well as commission that they are reliving repetitively, over and over again in these lesser realms.

So, while they have no literal means of reconciling their wrongs – at least, not in their own consciousness, see – because of this, they believe themselves lost, and they cry out, out of remorse, out of pain, some out of frustration and sadness, and all of these and associated emotions as you would know of them in the Earth... and there are other emotions (as you might call them such) of which you know not in the Earth because, for the most part, you have no way of experiencing them. Here is why: because they have gathered together according to like needs, like desires or limitations. Whether these be thought of as good or bad is irrelevant. They are one in intent and thought and emotion. It is this sense of oneness that predicates one of the major difficulties that causes them ultimately, every one, to lament.

No Way to Make Amends

There is no way for them, in their consciousness, to make amends, for the Earth is gone. Those with whom they interacted are gone, as well. If there is an addiction, they cannot obtain it: that which is the source of same, whether that be a chemical, or a situation in the Earth such as power and the need of same, or dominance and the need of same, or the need to *be* dominated... all of these can be as limitations, all of these can be addictions. So here, at first (upon arrival in these realms of consciousness, so to say), these newly arrived souls might find some degree of affinity, if not, curiously, some comfort in being with entities of like-mind, like-need and, sadly, like-limitation.

There are others who don't even make it to the Sea of Faces; these are considered Earthbound souls, and they might walk about the Earth constantly besieging those they feel they have wronged to forgive them, or constantly striving to fulfill their just-previous need while in physical body. These would be dealt with somewhat differently, as some of you know. But for now... Those who have moved beyond the Earth and who are with others of like-mind, so to say, in the Sea of Faces, are those who issued this call. What to do? How to deal with this? Why did this happen, in terms of the Channel's experience?

Opportunities of Service

According to the Channel's pledge of service, and according to his meditations and the desires of his heart and mind, he is seeking to fulfill those opportunities of service and bring to the Earth any such works as might be of value to those who he will leave behind upon his departure from same and his return here to rejoin us in these realms.

It is because of this intent, in no small degree, that he had the experience because, by having the experience it awakened him (and his colleague, whom he refers to as Ken) to this as a potential work, as a body of information which might be a resource for those who would seek it to understand the magnificent opportunity that a lifetime in the Earth presents; and that by looking at self openly, honestly, by looking at those things which each one adjudges to be wrong, which each one might adjudge to be an error: whether passive or active, omission or commission, both have the same end result and that is usually guilt, a feeling of remorse, a feeling of some varying degree of failure and/or loss. Indeed, very often the recognition of opportunities lost spawns greater guilt than actions of commission, see, in other words, those things which were done and are regretted.

When you can claim yourself, when you look into your heart and mind and take each of these things, which are as guilt or suppressed sadness or emotion, and you can claim them as your own—in other words, not deny them, not bury them deep within you—this helps. For in the case of the latter, all these things will be brought to the forefront upon departure from the Earth:

When Departing the Earth

The power, the determination, the energy which you give them, in terms of denial, reverses itself in a... in a sort of expression upon departure from the Earth; for when you leave

45

the Earth you leave behind the physical, but you do take with you all those deeds of kindness, all those deeds of support and encouragement. These are, in essence, converted to spiritual light. There are, more often than not, also those deeds which are neutral, where you didn't truly lose but then neither did you gain, and so these are as simply neutral energies. They neither add to the light nor detract from it. That is your spiritual level of acceptance. And then, of course, there are those deeds, faults, fears, guilt, and on and on, which are without light. See?

So, to give you an idea of what it is like for some souls when they depart from the Earth:

There is a sort of automatic equation which processes all of these events. Very many souls will tend to focus heavily upon those areas of their just-previous life wherein the light is absent. Those things which they have thrust to the deepest, darkest recesses of their being while in the Earth are upon the table of their transitional self in full view before themselves and those who are striving to serve them... guides, the Angelic Host, and so forth.

If these have been denied (which empowers the events, in a sense), then that must be dealt with before they can go on; unless, of course, they can know well enough to claim the light and to place the darkness only into a position of polarized balance so that they can see themselves more or less at arm's-length, spiritually. That by so doing they know that, while they might not equate themselves to have had a perfect lifetime, they will nonetheless accept the light that was present therein and move to the fullest extent that their sum and substance of spiritual light permits. Granted, they may not do this immediately to the fullest or highest level, but they will surely begin the process, and their movement will be continual—gradual for some, swiftly for others—but always moving.

Now those who, conversely, have significant items of darkness or absence of light upon the table of their transitional consciousness and who, upon experiencing same, wrap themselves with it in remorse and guilt, their very common thought is, "I cannot go before God or the Angelic Host. My sins are too great. My sorrow is too heavy. I will go elsewhere. rather than confront my shame, my remorse, my guilt, before God himself."

The guides, the Angelic Host, and so forth strive to reach out to them, to let them know that God is all-loving, and that these are just experiences, opportunities which, while they may have been missed or neglected or misused, are nonetheless only opportunities, only experiences, and not they, the soul, the Child of God themselves. See?

Potential Service

So then, as the Channel heard this lamenting, it was moreso the comparative emotional state and all that sort that he reacted to, perhaps, moreso than any audible cry (although we should concur this, too, he did hear). This, we know, has awakened him to the needs of those souls and to the potential service of those who are yet in the Earth consciousness to those groupings in the Sea of Faces... and to themselves as individuals, as groups, as classes and masses and peoples.

Let it begin with me. Let me be sent. Let me be used. These are good words. They are admirable. They are teachings according to the Master... indeed, to most all who are masters in the Earth, past, present, and future.

It is well, however, to remember what it is you are offering to God to use and send. Art thou the vessel of truth? Or are you burdened with your own suppressed and hidden (hidden from self) sadness, remorse, guilt, or (by your evaluation) sins?

It is thought and taught by some that one way to purge self of these (in other words to make amends) is to go out in service. We can and do concur with this to the extent that those guilts are not so deeply buried within you that not even a wondrous work of the Christ light, of God's very Light Itself, can reach into the depths of where you have placed these, and illuminate them and free you from them.

CLOSING COMMENTS

If you want to fix something that is broken in the Earth, do you hide it away and attempt to fix it at a distance? Or do you place it in the center of your repair table and focus good, bright, lighting upon it so that you can examine it carefully (minutely, if necessary) and see what the need of repair is? And then look for the tools and the materials that are needed to make the repair, that that thing might be good again, that it might be functional and well and do good service thereafter?

How is it any different with things of the heart? With thoughts of your emotion? With those things which you consider to be misdeeds or non-deeds? Put them on the table of your life itself. Claim them. They're just another broken thing or malfunctioning thing, aren't they? Aren't these simply aspects of your life and your potential, which you now see as less than desirable to you?

You have the power to change these; but not by hiding them away, not by placing them into the depths of your being where they shall grow in their condition of imbalance until such time as your transition, whereupon you will re-live them. Better that you should, from the consciousness and from the support of your spiritual group and such, look at them while yet in the Earth. You can fix them. You can make them well and whole. You can balance them out. You can claim power over them. Do not give them power over you.

Begin by praying for those who have gone on. Begin, as well, by not holding thoughts of debt or indebtedness, by not holding thoughts of anger and remorse, but placing them into an appropriate position of balance, of judgment and evaluation, and nothing more.

The Cry of the Lost is very real. Your prayers will help them. Your light and your works will be a light and works on their behalf, as well, even if but only in portion, see?

And love that part of *you* which may, at the moment, also be lost. If you hear a cry from within your being, answer it. Bring it out. Bring it into the light of God, and let His for-

48

giveness and love correct it. Let Him *fix it* (see, given with loving humor).

May the grace and blessings of our Father's wisdom ever be that lamp to guide your footsteps. Fare thee well then for the present, dear friends. Om Shanti.

READING FOUR: *ACCEPTING THE LIGHT*

AL MINER/CHANNEL: This is June 6, 1998. This is a request for a topical research reading entitled, *Sea of Faces, Part IV*. I want to thank my dear friend who has requested this reading and sponsored it. The questions and commentary that I am about to read have been submitted by him as well. He writes as follows:

QUESTIONS

Lama Sing: Thank you for your readings on the Sea of Faces. This is a request for another topical reading on the same subject. Most of these questions are derived from questions Nancy (transcriber for the Lama Sing readings) sent to the Channel. And the questions are as follows:

If we go to the Sea of Faces when we leave the Earth, do we feel transported there, or is it like a birth? Once we are there, do we remember that we have not always been there? Or is there amnesia for our past?

Can you elaborate more on how an entity in the Sea of Faces is able to change their circumstances? How do they receive knowledge that there are other opportunities for them and that they can move to higher realms? How do they let the light in? Is there some system by which they have access to that knowledge so that they can spiritually progress?

What are the ramifications of there being so many thousands of entities stuck in the Sea of Faces or lesser realms? Does this make an imbalance in the universe? It has been said that we must all return to God together. If that is so, how does this affect the process?

When we pray for "all those who are dwelling in some darkness and for whom there are none in joyful prayer", does this help them one at a time? Or are we able to affect groups all at one time?

If we go to the Sea of Faces, does that mean that our Earthly guides go there also? Do they have a choice of staying or going on to other works? Will new guides that specialize in Sea of Faces entities take over? (That's an interesting question.) Or is the dedication of our Earth lifetime guides so great that they stay with us no matter how long it takes for us to awaken?

Are there other realms, besides the Earth, in which we are "born", have a lifetime, and "die"? Or when we go to other realms, are we in a spirit body that does not have a life cycle and which does not age?

Various sources have said that we can have lifetimes on other planets, such as Venus. This does not appear to be physical life, so it must be a spiritual sojourn. Does the Sea of Faces have anything to do with life associated with other planets, perhaps like Saturn? What is an experience on one of these planets for?

Thank you, Nancy, Al, and Lama Sing, for your continued work with us in the Earth. Blessings to you all.

LAMA SING COMMENTARY

Yes, we have the Channel then and, as well, those references which apply to the topic now before us.

We welcome your questions as a continuum of works on this most worthy of topics.

OPENING COMMENTS

Before we commence, we should comment briefly: Be aware of the literal fact that you are, in the current of their lifetime in the Earth plane, building your future; that which shall follow you upon departure from the Earth through the process called death is that which you are building, living, believing, in the present. So it is our humble prayer that these works which are being performed by those of you in the Earth who have embraced this understanding, and we here and elsewhere who have rallied to this call offering it as information, serves as a light to make The Way passable for those who shall follow.

Turning to your questions, we have the following information as has been brought forward in response to your queries.

TO AND FROM THE SEA OF FACES

Upon departure from the Earth, should it be that your destination is such as called the Sea of Faces, then it would probably occur as the result moreso of an attraction, rather than anything like a birth or even in the sense of being transported there.

Those who find themselves within the Sea of Faces generally do not recognize it, literally, as such. Rather, they are aware of the fact that they are in a realm of consciousness and among other entities whose thoughts, whose attitudes, and yes, whose limitations, are similar to, if not identical to, their own.

Arriving

So it is that the movement there is more likened unto an escape, an avoidance, of what many of them know to be movement to a greater realm; perhaps, yes, even to the very throne of God, or so they would surmise within. It is their reluctance to face God or to face the Light that so often is at the basis of their being limited and/or finding themselves in the Sea of Faces. As the intent of your question implies, it could be thought of in some obscure ways as a birth of sorts, for departure from the Earth is, in fact, a birth into a different way of life.

The differentiation between the true re-birth into the spiritual form and beyond, and that of those who are found in the Sea of Faces, is that they are unwilling to let the process unfold or continue because of the reasons we have given just above and, to be sure, many others as well, some of which we will touch on, we believe, as we progress here.

Remaining

Once an entity is there in the Sea of Faces, very often with the passage of their experiences, they lose the concept of a past in the complete sense. So it is like an amnesia of sorts, but many of these entities bring this on themselves. They try to force out of their consciousness memories of the lifetime just past, with the exception (very often) of those things which are the very bonds that keep them in the Sea of Faces.

An example might be that an entity will not remember any good deeds that they may have performed while previously in the Earth, these being heavily overshadowed by feelings of guilt, remorse, feelings of pain, belief that they have neglected or failed some calling; and, of course, some obsession or addiction, if you will, to something that is Earthly in its orientation. Let us be quick to comment here that the use of the term *addiction* in this context can embrace virtually anything you can think of in addition to addiction to narcotics or something similar; entities of great number are in the Sea of Faces because they are addicted to something that would seem obscure to the thinking of those of you who hear these works. Control, power, authority, these are all addictive forces.

But what of the opposites! Some entities are addicted to subservience. Some cry out to be guided, to be led, in fact, need to be dominated. Others are addicted to a calling, and that could be literally any vocation or avocation in the Earth plane consciousness. While usually such entities are more easily awakened, some can be steadfast in their need for a continuum of the previous experiences in the Earth, in order for them to feel worthy or appropriate.

Again, this could seem from the Earth very difficult to comprehend, but if you contemplate it just briefly and look around, think about it, you'll probably come to the realization that there are entities you know of who categorically fit just those descriptions. (See? Lovingly given.)

Generally speaking, the longer an entity (by the measure of Earth time) dwells in the Sea of Faces, the less they remember of their past, with the exception of those things which they are intensely focused upon and are the bonds that keep them in the Sea of Faces.

Leaving

Entities in the Sea of Faces can actually change their circumstances in what you would call in the Earth "the twinkling of an eye." In fact, it is remarkable if not amazing, that circumstances are, once again, those which these entities themselves support and contribute to.

THE SEA OF FACES STRUCTURE

As we have given previously, the Sea of Faces is vast and virtually unlimited, as is all of existence, for that matter; but in the Sea of Faces there are varying strata or what could be called realms *within* the Sea of Faces.

Realms Within the Sea of Faces

These various realms are generally inhabited by entities of like-thought, like-attitude and, unfortunately, similar limitations. This is due to what is referred to so often as that called Universal Law. Entities can move to the level of their own spiritual acceptance and not beyond.

It would be no different than a mountain climber in the Earth able to climb only so high under their own power and, at a certain point, requiring a supplement of oxygen and other utilitarian things in order to progress further. So, imagine an entity moving in a direction (which you would assess to be similar to the mountain climber), that is, upwards toward the Light. Their capacity to spiritually breathe determines how far, how high, and to what level, they can ascend. That's, of course, an analogy, an example, but we think it graphic sufficient to provide understanding (this shall be our prayer). To change the circumstance, then, clearly requires that they are able to breathe at less dense levels... or to accept (which is the implied reference meant by *breathing*, here) greater spiritual awareness. We could say that the more unlimited an entity is, the more unlimited is their potential for ascension.

Now bear in mind here we are using the terms "ascension" and "movement upwards" advisedly. They are not literally relevant, for there is no literal up or down. There is consciousness, and that is demarcated for your understanding in a level format: layers, progressive ones, moving from the Earth upwards and outwards to the "higher, more spiritual realms". Thinking, then, of Universal Consciousness – God Consciousness, if you will – as being one of those destinations which is of the Light and demarcating this as, let us say, the Seventh Major Realm (and the Earth being in the approximate midst of the Third Major Realm), you can see that there is some distance, for in each major realm there are seven sub-realms, and within those, other sub-realms. In fact, this could be thought of, in essence, as an unlimited structure within itself, and that is literally true.

Fear of the Light

Entities in the Sea of Faces do have within them that same light which is within the Greatest of All. But it is dimmed, obscured, veiled, if you will, by their own thoughts, their own attitudes, their own limitations. This is why we have said the more unlimited one is spiritually and the greater is their ability to accept in an unlimited manner, the higher is their potential progression upon departure from the Earth.

So, if these entities have that same Light within them as those in greater realms, why does it not shine forth? What are these veils, these coverings, those things which block the Light from manifesting? To answer that is to answer the nature of Consciousness, Itself, the nature of entities in the Earth and virtually in all realms.

It is quite simply answered in this way: If you ask, it is given. If you seek, you shall find; but if you do not ask and neither do you seek, your consciousness, obviously, is focused elsewhere. If you are facing a light, it is very bright and beautiful; but if you turn your back to it, you perhaps only see shadows, believing these to be all that is, when Truth is immediately behind you.

To let the Light in (or out, more accurately, given with a note of loving humor) involves a system of knowledge, which

55

you have in a part of your question, that they always have access to. For the most part, they do not seek it. In fact, many in those realms called the Sea of Faces hide from it, run from it, and, yes, even fear it. They fear judgment. They fear being known for who and what they believe themselves to be. They cannot believe that their sins, their faults, their flaws, their wrongdoing, could ever be forgiven. They are unwilling to accept assistance from those entities of light and are unwilling to receive those whom they love or have loved who have gone beyond and those who loved them. They are embarrassed, they are sad, they are angry, they are bitter, and most all other similar terms that you can conceive of. These and more will be found as attitudes and emotions borne within and held and manifested by entities in the Sea of Faces.

WAYS TO HELP

The way to let the Light in, the way to change their circumstances, and the way for them to become enlightened, is to wait for them to ask.

They Must Ask

Remembering Universal Law, and one of the primary laws—the Right of Free Will—can bring about an understanding of why great beings of Light who are entirely capable of swooping into these realms, radiating the light of their love and forgiveness from God, do not and cannot, for they serve God. And to serve God is to serve and uphold His Law. So the right of Free Will, one of the most powerful of all Universal Laws, is like the proverbial double-edged sword, in the sense that it cuts for goodness and limitation alike. It cleaves, dimensionally, those who believe in their own limitation from the Light.

Help Through Prayer

But there is a way and several of them, and one such is based upon this same Law. For these entities have, in their most recent past, departed from the Earth and have ended up in this realm (or composite of realms) called the Sea of Faces, which is in close proximity and affinity with the Earth. Therefore, according to the Law, those who are in the consciousness of Earth can interact with the Sea of Faces, and the Law is upheld.

For, for sake of discussion here, the Sea of Faces is a part of the Earth. It is what one could call only a step or two apart from same. In the literal sense, both the Sea of Faces and the Earth occupy the same time and space—one in three-dimensional form, the other in extra-dimensional form (in other words that which is beyond the finite). So, as there would be one or more in the Earth who offer their prayer and offer works for those who are in the Sea of Faces, then this is a powerful method of assisting those who have lost their sight and dwell therein.

We know that there will be a myriad of questions on that general comment, and to anticipate some of them, we offer the following:

Because the *vibrations* (if we might call them such) of those of you who are in the Earth plane in physical body and those who are in the Sea of Faces are very similar, and because the thought-forms which are the construct of the Sea of Faces are generally those which are drawn from and supported by the Earth itself, you can interact with them, and they with you, and the Law is not violated. You can, deliberately, as individuals— but far better, as a grouping—intentionally set about works for those who are in the Sea of Faces, those who have lost their way, and you can help to make the way passable for them.

There are many variations to such a work, and many methodologies that can be employed to accomplish this. One of the first as is known in the Earth, and perhaps the most powerful, is to offer your prayer; but as some of you have realized and taken some action to respond to, it is difficult to pray for those in the Sea of Faces when you do not know who they are. You may perhaps not know their names, the source of their limitations, and for that matter have any idea how to approach them.

So you offer your prayers, as we do as we opened these works and other such works: stating that "We offer these prayers in the names of all those for whom there are none in joyful prayer."

So, supposing that there are entities—which, in fact, there are—who do not have anyone left in the Earth who even remembers them... Think about that! Think about the effect this must have on those entities. Those whom they have interacted with have long ago passed on. Those times which, perhaps, they had some affinity to, those events and circumstances, the very structure of the society in which they dwelled, all this and more has long since faded into history. Think about that. Think about where it would place just one of these souls who, perhaps, was a fallen Viking, one who fell in battle in the French Revolution, a frontiers-person who lost their life traveling west, one in Europe defending a castle and their family and their way of life fallen perhaps to dis-ease and not an enemy, or to starvation being under siege. While the castle might remain, naught else is evident in the Earth.

So it could be said such souls as these could truly be described (and appropriately so) as *lost*. It is for such souls, such entities, that our prayer is, to the uttermost, given: those who will not be remembered this day in the Earth by someone who loved, who cared, who interacted with them. See?

What does this prayer do? What does *your* prayer do? What other works can you and your groupings perform? You can do just as we've described, and you can open yourselves, and you'll be heard.

Help Through Dream and Meditation

You can go where angels cannot, in the sense of helping them; even though an angel might stand at the side of one of these entities who are lost, they may see them not, for their sight cannot conceive of such a being. In your meditations, in your dreams, many of you may recall oddities of events, seemingly those which have no correlation to the Earth in its present time. Those of you who may record these may find that, more often than not, during the course of a fortnight or such you've had one or more such dreams.

Consider for a moment that, in your spiritual form, perhaps you have gone to these realms; and since you are of the Earth (even though in the moment not *in* it), you can pass through these realms with very little disruption to them. In fact, most all of these realms in the Sea of Faces will accept your presence. *In fact*, they might seek you out! Should there be concern here for self? Not really. They cannot harm you, even though some are quite intimidating in their manner, in their bearing, and perhaps even in their intent to intimidate you; but they have no power in and of themselves. So long as you know this (and even if you do not), upon awakening, they will only be a memory, and perhaps a fleeting and vague one at that.

If you give your dreams some awareness, and if you prepare prior to sleep with a very simple prayer (choose your own words, choose your own thoughts), and then as you enter into the sleep, perhaps your spirit will come before them and help them. See?

Sea of Faces' Effects On Others

The ramifications of there being such a goodly number of entities in the general Sea of Faces is significant. Are other souls blocked in their progression because of them and their number? Not really.

Can we return to God, even though they are still dwelling in this collective expression called the Sea of Faces? Yes. Will we be complete upon so doing? No.

How does the Sea of Faces', seemingly and literally so, ever-increasing number of entities who dwell therein, affect the process of our return to God? Herein is a considerable commentary that could be given:

You are correct in that, even though we can individually return unto oneness with God, we shall come to know a sense (this is not the appropriate word, but it's all we have to give you), a sense of sadness, a sense of loneliness or lone*some*ness for others who we love, brethren who are in lesser realms, entities, many of them, who just might be in the Sea of Faces.

It is that, upon reaching a state of oneness with God that we come to know such a joy, such a wonder, and so many other experiences that are indescribable in mere words, but we also come to know that this joy is incomplete, this wonder is only partial in its potential because it isn't shared with all souls, because there are others who are limited, who are dwelling in some sadness or darkness (albeit so often, if not always, self-imposed).

So is it then that you find entities of great Light, souls of wondrous majesty, of beauty, of grace, of love and compassion, who leave the Greater Realms, taking on all manner of works—and even incarnations, physically, in lesser realms—with the hope and prayer that, by so doing, they can contribute to making the way passable for those who shall follow. This is the Work. This is that which is the gift of the Christ. This is that Light which burns eternally within each soul, be it great or small in its luminosity.

So, does this make an imbalance in the universe? Perhaps it could be rightfully stated, yes, actually; for those in the Light will seek out, ever, those who are not.

But those who are in the Earth have the greater opportunity to help those who are in the Sea of Faces, as obscure as that might seem to you, as illogical as it might sound.

Help from Earth Is Most Effective

Consider this: Which is the better to help build a structure from wood in the Earth, a carpenter or a poet? Who, then, should be sought out to write a beautiful sonnet to honor someone's accomplishments in the Earth, a carpenter or a poet? If we have four entities, two who are on a seashore and two who are out at sea in a large rowboat, which of the four are able to move the boat? The two on shore can call out suggestions and urgings. They can call out instructions. But in the end, only the two who are in the boat can do the rowing. Think of the Sea of Faces and the Earth as being in the same boat (given with a note of loving humor). See this, then?

When you pray *for those who are dwelling in some darkness and for whom there are none in joyful prayer*, as we do at the onset of works such as this, it is akin to broadcasting a radio program in the Earth plane. The broadcast may go out to all lands and all peoples within the radius of its strength (the sending station), but only those who tune their radio receiver's frequency to that which is being broadcast can actually hear the program. The others will walk about and do what they are normally doing, oblivious for the most part that we are even broadcasting a program; but those who are attuned will receive it. That is how that prayer works.

We do also know the nature of so many in the Sea of Faces, and we know that they are sort of continually scanning various frequencies (using the analogy of broadcasts again) looking for something, often they know not what, but many of them are looking for some way to fulfill themselves. So, knowing this nature, and knowing that they are seeking—from the Earth, see, and not from the higher realms—know that your prayers of that nature will likely be received by many in the Sea of Faces. Whether they continue to listen and receive the blessings of the prayers you offer, and whether or not they are willing to release limitation and go on is, of course, according to their free-will choice. But the moreso the prayer is offered, or works similar to such, the greater is the probability, the percentage of probability, that many shall be helped. Some entities in the Sea of Faces need so little to go on and yet cannot find it. So you are able to help, certainly, one or more, or even groups. See?

But you must also be given this information, so we are told here:

Change the Earth and Change the Sea of Faces
The energies, the thoughts, the emotions, the habits, and all those sorts of things that are in the Earth consciousness, are just those things that the majority of entities in the Sea of Faces want. Until these, as a source of fulfillment to the entities in the Sea of Faces have been changed, they will continually look to

the Earth for the fulfillment, the satiation, or satisfaction, of their desire.

Granted, they have no physical body with which to experience, as they did while in the Earth. Still, even the tiniest fragment is sought after, if it can be found, in terms of that which is their limitation. See?

Yes, you are able to affect groups at one time—sometimes greatly, sometimes not so much so. It doesn't always have to do with what you do or how you do it, but the receptivity, the readiness, of those who perceive and/or receive the blessings of your prayers.

Our prayers (to answer an unspoken question) from here are, for the most part, not received by them; some, yes, but not in the manner as prayers from the Earth. It might be asked, why do we offer these prayers through the Channel as we have done for so many Earth years past? The answer will be obvious for some. Nonetheless… It is because the Channel is in the Earth and, as we speak through him as (if you will) an instrument of these works, it is thereafter made manifest in the consciousness of Earth.

So the Channel (and yourselves, as you hear this) reflect the power of the prayer which we offer from the Earth to the Sea of Faces… and we thank you for your kindness in that regard in the past, in the present, and in those future works which we know many of you shall do.

Guides in the Sea of Faces

If you go to the Sea of Faces, those who are with you as guides in the Earth plane remain with you once you depart through the veil of separateness or the portal called death.

They do remain with you, for the most part (or the majority of them) throughout. (Some do not, for others, as your questions have implied, who are much more adept in some manner or another at helping those in the Sea of Faces, might take their place.)

But for the most part, your guides sustain a contact with

you until you are conscious of them. That is when the guides' work is considered complete. Some will remain with you thereafter, some will not. You may go on to serve in your own capacity as helpmeets to others, as guides or many other variants of same; or you may go on for further (you could rightfully call it) study and growth on your own; but always, those who are progressing in spiritual consciousness have someone or (in many instances) *several* entities who are with them. So, yes, if you go to the Sea of Faces, initially at least, your Earthly guides will go there also.

The Nature of a Guide's Work

You asked if they have a choice. Certainly. All entities always have choices. But remember that guides who are with you in the Earth plane are with you because they have chosen this, usually out of a bond created in the past or out of love. According to Universal Law, they wish to give to you some great blessing in return for a blessing you have given to them. Or they could be souls of Light who know you and who know of your progression, and also know that their knowledge, their wisdom, can provide you perhaps just one more step or two, that you can break free from the *Wheel of Life* (as it's called): the cycle of incarnations in the Earth. Very often, entities who are about to make significant spiritual progress will have many entities with them. It isn't so much so that you need that much help to progress the last few steps; but these entities (many of them) are with you as an honor, as a gift to *the guides*, and as an opportunity for them to learn along with you.

If you perceive an entity in the Earth with a goodly number of entities about them, you can generally conclude this is one who is either in the Earth plane to do a goodly work in God's name, to contribute to making the Way passable, or one who is about to progress into the greater Light and wisdom of God.

There are some instances where those who are not so conscious, not so progressed, might have large numbers of guides, but these are usually only temporary and are event-oriented rather than soul-level orientation. (That is also a complex area that could justifiably receive considerable comment, should there be an interest in the Earth plane.)

Let us conclude with this area of questioning very clearly, so that there is no question, no doubt...

We know of no entity in the Sea of Faces who is without a guide. Entities in the Sea of Faces are given considerable attention. There are beautiful efforts which take place on their behalf, and new works (we are told) are forthcoming in that regard, as certain entities come forth to bear the light in unique ways unto their needs.

As an addendum here, you may find it of interest, if not curiosity, that entities who are newly departed from the Earth very often make some of the very best guides and teachers to those who are in the Sea of Faces. The perhaps obvious reason for this is that their consciousness (their memory, if you will) and their awareness of the Earth and its influences is still very clear and very timely.

Other Realms and Pure Consciousness

Yes, there are other realms in which you can be ".," have a lifetime, and "die." There are other realms in which you can have a form; not specifically physical but, for all intents and purposes, those who inhabit those forms come to know them, to believe them, and to live in them, just every bit like you do in the Earth, believing that your physical body *is* your body. There are structures of consciousness which follow the very same patterns as do those which predicate the Wheel of Life (or the cycle of incarnations in the Earth) and, yet, which are not manifest to your physical sight, dimensionally, but are every bit as real to those who inhabit same, just as your bodies are real to you.

Some of these are, yes, in and about that which you call your planet and other spheres and other galaxies and other universes of which you haven't even a perception of in the present. Only in the last several Earth years has there been any general acceptance that such is possible. There are expressions of matter that are every bit as real as your matter but which are not in your dimensional comprehension. They are, for the most part, the *mirror* of your own expression; and therefore, as you are mirrored in finiteness, this is the polarity to your finiteness, and the expression has the same end result.

Then you can move to other dimensions (other levels, if you will) where the same parallax, matrix, or paradox, can be found to be true. See? When you go to other realms, generally speaking, we believe that you would call that body a *spirit body*, if only because it doesn't conform to what you call a physical body under the dictums of your definition of same. But you are perceiving your physical body from the Earth... from *within* it; only those who can get outside of their physical body can perceive it from the spiritual perspective or the more *eternal* perspective.

Imagine, then, if you left your physical body and looked back at it, it would seem different, somehow a bit more removed from you. Perhaps with time and experience, it might even seem foreign to you. And the moreso you projected yourself (perhaps *astrally* is an acceptable term here), the moreso would you begin to look upon your astral body as your real body and the other as only a shell. Well, imagine that times one thousand or a greater number, and you can see how very quickly the astral body can become the spiritual body... which can become the etheric body... and so on and so forth; with transitions taking place with remarkable fluidity, each one successively, ultimately becoming that body in which you exist. When, in fact, you are *none* of these and *all* of them, for you are infinite.

You are Consciousness, which may or may not express itself as form. It is Consciousness with which you feel the thoughts, the emotions, and such, which come from others. It is Consciousness with which you travel... you reach out to embrace or to think or conceive of something. It is Consciousness of which mind builds, drawing upon emotion, drawing upon memory, as the very substances of which mind builds.

You can go to other realms and be in what you call a spirit body. And some of these realms do have a cycle very similar to what you consider to be a life cycle. And some realms have an aging process. Some realms of consciousness within the Sea of Faces have these to such an extent that entities who have dwelled therein have been born therein over and over and over again. Some know this; some have come to be aware of the fact that they are beginning yet another sojourn in this very same realm. Very often, it is the tedium, the boredom, and the sense of a longing to be greater than this that helps to break them free. It is in that moment wherein they ask, wherein they call out, that the Light can enter and re-kindle their inner light to its fullness.

Sojourns in other realms, sojourns in and about other planetary expressions, are very often aligned similarly to what you know of in the Earth as astrological influences or tendencies. Those aspects as are generally aligned to the planets as you perceive them from the Earth, and as are relevant to what you call astrological influences, are, on occasion, used by entities in the Sea of Faces for varying purpose.

Often, those who guide will work to bring entities from the Sea of Faces to other realms, to other dimensions, to other planetary expressions; that by so doing, an entity from the Sea of Faces is confronted with their own limitation or may see the counterpart to that, the polarity, the parallax, the matrix. See?

Planetary sojourns are used to gain awareness in certain areas, certain characteristics; sometimes to better equip a soul who is preparing to re-enter the Earth, that they might make the better progress while therein, or that experiences in the other planetary expressions might better equip them to accomplish a work, as such entities incarnate for benevolent purpose; and so on and so forth.

You could think of the planetary efforts on the part of guides and those who are in the Sea of Faces as a hospital of sorts, which is categorized by the condition of limitation or disease, as defined in and about the Earth. But in the wisdom that the guide possesses, they might discern that a sojourn here on

Venus will awaken some aspect of love or compassion, or some eternal life essence. Or that Jupiter or Mars will bring about, face-to-face, the block, the limitation, the aggression, or the weakness, that is in an entity's consciousness. And so on and so forth, you see. (Again, not unlike your knowledge of the astrological influence upon an entity as they enter.)

So an experience on any one of these planets or in other realms or other spheres is for the opportunity that this offers to such entities, and they are not done idly. It is with great care, great wisdom, and often with considerable counsel, that an entity will sojourn within or about one such.

We are advised here that we must conclude soon for this present meeting.

CLOSING COMMENTS

Let us state to you in an attitude of what we'll call loving cooperation, if you can reach out to others who are in need, know that simultaneously you are helping self.

First, we encourage you to know yourselves: to know who you are, to open self to love, that you hold within yourself an attitude of love for self, as contrary as that might sound to tradition. For what you seek outwardly from God, from The Christ, is also within you. And it is to this essence of uniqueness—which is you and only you; the beauty, the wonder therein—that we encourage you to love as God loves you, and The Christ as well.

The light of The Christ is not intangible. Nor is it mystical or magical. And yet, it is all of these and greater. This is what is within you. And this is what is worthy of your love! Not the little self-love, but the Great Self-love. The little self will receive love from the Self with the capital "S", and the little self and the Greater Self will, thereafter, become as one. One is not destroyed to elevate the other; they become one. See?

Once again, we express our profound humbleness for this opportunity of service with you, and these worthy works performed in God's name.

And so it shall ever be our prayer, and it shall be so written here, as we ask...

May the grace and blessings of our Father's wisdom ever be that lamp which guides your footsteps.

Fare thee well then for the present, dear friends. Om Shanti. The peace of God ever be with thee and upon thee. Amen.

Part Two:

A Collection of Excerpts

Like Begets Like

Those realms very close to the Earth, often referred to by this Channel as the Sea of Faces... many of those entities therein dwell in eternal darkness. They prefer it. It was their time of activity while in the Earth plane... their preferred time; therefore, their realm is dark. Many other souls dwell in a realm of darkness created by their fear, their anger, their hostility, or by a habit of a sort.

Other realms are comprised of souls who prefer to have the mirror image of existence in the Earth, and for all respects it is a duplicate existence of the Earth except that no injury, no harm, no dis-ease is ever permanent; one may go through the effects, the emotions, the results of same, but it never endures... eventually the subject entity who is enduring the pain of such finds themselves whole again, and then repeats the process if that is their need. Some realms' entities do the same with guilt, with sorrow, and others do the same with anger or acts of violence. Like begets like. Realms of violence are inhabited by entities who need same in order to break free of the illusion.

Other Realms
January 26, 1988

How the Sea of Faces Beckons

As one moves before the massive array of influences, of potentials, each color [each encountered layer or sub-realm] is as an offering, in essence saying, "See me, here I am... a realm of existence, wonderful... I'll provide your every wish... Look about you... there are entities here... They think as you do... Join them... Come with us."

That's the kind of influence that's present in the Sea of Faces. It's that sort of thing that is dealt with.

Peter Project
April 11, 1990

Limited by Self-Judgment

Realms close to the Earth are those realms of existence wherefrom or wherein entities bound to the Earth dwell, often burdened by the most unlikely thought-forms or desires. There are those among those realms who are, as history will recount them, of great spiritual import and purity, and yet they dwell in that realm the Channel calls *The Sea of Faces*... because of their own self-judgment, their own feeling of failure, or of having "sinned" in some certain way.

Attunement Project

March 27, 1986

Possessed

The circumstances of *possession* is a very broad topic and should not be treated in any degree of casual commentary.

No soul can truly possess (in other words, take over) another soul without that soul's permission in one way or another. There can often be the appearance of possession, but upon close investigation, this is merely a very powerful influencing force... the influencing of other souls who have abandoned their own free will, their hope, their ideal, their purpose, their goal, or who are in some way addicted.

All those qualities of emotion as you might categorically define them such as jealousy, anger, or even lust, grief, and so forth, can and do act as a sort of magnetic polarization attracting entities from the Sea of Faces.

This attraction, generally, would have no effect upon the entity experiencing those emotions or psychological manifestations, unless this were to be a consistent pattern or to become a way of life. In other words, if an entity dwells constantly in an attitude of rage, or in an attitude of lust constantly, then surely, entities of like-intent or desire may very well dwell in close proximity to that entity, because they are attempting to experience the effect of those actions by someone in physical body.

Can they cause trouble? Certainly, because they act as a cloud around that entity who is enraged, and prevent them from, by the presence of the cloud, perceiving the light. But when the rage passes, these entities will be flooded with light. Or if prayer is involved here for the entity who is enduring this traumatic emotion, that is a light as well, and will dispel any influence from entities of the Sea of Faces.

Peter Project
February 19, 1993

Thoughts Attract

Like attracts, and so where they can find those things that satiate their needs, even if they are second-hand, as you colloquially call it, they will do so. They *must* try, no matter what! They have sought to dominate one another and, finding that this is an eternal cycle that begins and ends and begins and ends, over and over again, they are turning to other places... other entities in the Earth.

Thoughts attract... attitudes, emotions, actions, all attract entities of like-intent. And even though an entity might mean well—in the sense of not causing harm or not dominating—if they adopt involuntarily, so to say, such attitudes, they can attract these entities from what could be called the Sea of Faces or such as this, who seek to sort of fill their appetite for such by associating with such actions.

Fortunately, those who are well-intended and might have only a momentary outburst of such, out of frustration or whatnot, repel these entities easily. They are only there momentarily. But where this has become a way of life or habit for some, in other instances these entities can be found thickly expressed around them.

Peter Project
May 28, 1992

The Non-Seeker

The non-seeker not only will not perceive nor hear, but will more likely *deny* truth when it's presented them, because they have become comfortable with their realm of expression. To them, the void, or point of demarcation between levels of growth, constitutes the outer reach of existence. In short, there is nothing else but who they are and where they are. Upon departing from the Earth, many of these fall into a deep comatose or sleep-like state, choosing to become more fully conscious only upon return to the Earth. Variations upon this constitute those souls who occupy the *Sea of Faces*.

It is as easy for a zealous preacher to be bound to the Earth as it is the alcoholic... both have a "lust." See? (Humbly and lovingly given.)

Personal Reading
April 8, 1990

Influencing the "Lesser Realms"

You have perhaps considered this [the Sea of Faces] to be a sphere enveloping the Earth, whereupon one might think, no matter, moving away from the Earth, they must pass through this realm. That is quite accurate. But also understand that these in the Sea of Faces also have their own realms.

If you would, think of them then (in the graphic depiction) as being the underpinnings of the Earth, wherein they exist beneath you in the sense that yours is a certain level of spiritual acceptance, and theirs is just so another, and beneath them another, and beneath them another, and so forth.

Example: Here's a realm which underlies the Earth in terms of spiritual acceptance: It is very dark, brownish in color, and it has very bestial energies. The energies are those of survival and aggression. *As above, so below.* Well then, where there are those fuels of thought-forms that precipitate down to these realms, these are substances from which these entities can perpetuate their realm. To a degree, then, they are somewhat dependent upon those of you in the Earth consciousness for their existence.

In the Earth plane you are controlling your thinking, your emotion, based upon experience and knowledge; as you gain more information, you more or less correlate this all together, and it forms a collage of who and what you are. In this realm, however, much of the salient qualities of that result are filtered out by the intervening *veils*; and as such, this realm receives *only* those things as are of aggression and primordial or bestial intent for its sustenance.

It should be noted that, in this realm, while one might attack another brutally, in short order the victim arises completely well and the whole fracas starts again... over and over. They steal from one another. They covet. They lay in waiting to attack one another... first one, then the other, and so it goes. Until such time as one of them might call out to be free, at which point they are guided upwards.

All of your thoughts are like fodder, like nourishment; the greater is *your* hostility, your animosity, your aggression, your hatred, the greater is the power of *their* realm. Your prayers and your efforts to purify the overriding thought-form of your realm, as you can see from this commentary, can do much to help those beneath you. You are the light above the realms beneath you, just as perhaps you might see [guides] as lights in realms above you... if they were angry and spiteful and coveted things, that would be the light emanating to you.

One of the difficulties that has been experienced in these lesser realms in the recent time of the Earth has been the abandonment of conscious thought on the part of many entities through various mechanisms or means. What you call narcotics or drugs is one of the major culprits here. It is providing great quantities of energy, raw energy, for these entities and those in the Sea of Faces collectively to, in essence, nourish themselves, to fortify, to strengthen, to broaden their realm. So while you are thinking of serving those in your realm, each time you serve

74

one in your realm, you have perhaps served ten or twenty in realms beneath you, as called, also, the Sea of Faces.

Peter Project

December 6, 1990

By Invitation Only

One of the qualities that you would find sorely lacking in what is called the Sea of Faces is the quality of joy, for those things which limit these entities from attaining their true joyful potential are but memories; they are shadows upon the potential of the soul's own light. And until these can be cast aside, that light does not shine as it is intended to so do.

So as there is darkness in the heart, mind, or spirit of an entity—be they inhabiting a physical body or not—then there will always be that which follows thereafter as a sort of reactory condition that seeks to bring forth the light and to provide a state of balance and harmony thereabouts.

The entities in the Sea of Faces do not have carnal, physical bodies. They are not incarnate; they are discarnate... out of physical expression. Therefore, while they—*by their choice*—still dwell within the periphery of the Earth's influence and the massive energy fields of some of the thought-forms, they do not have the expressed right of free will and such that is a part of the Earth itself and the Earth's structure (that is, not physical structure, but spiritual, mental and emotional structure). Therefore, they can only enter in where they are, in a manner of speaking (quote) "invited" (end quote).

Now the invitation is not, as such, a knowledgeable one, wherein an entity in the Earth sits down and begins the process of inviting entities to join them from the Sea of Faces. Although it has occurred, and does, it is not what you would call the normal sequence or order of things.

It is, rather, by the involuntary actions, so to say, or the relinquishing of one's lawful right of Free Will, that such entities can and do have an impact upon those who are indulging in

75

habits of their own desire.

Peter Project
July 26, 1994

Freed into the Embrace

There are many souls whose focus is so intense upon what was in their life just previous in the Earth that they cannot see or accept that they could be more than this. So, those who have, through various means and activities, reached a point where just one whit more might open them to forgive themselves enough to go on, then these works and these workers will do just that.

"Lord, grant me Thy grace. Help Thou me to release that which limits me. I long to be with Thee. I hear the song of Thy spirit. Claim me, Father, as Thine, as I now claim you as my Father." ...In the moment that is stated, the way is passable for them, and there is rejoicing, great celebration.

Where do they go? Each to that which is unto their own acceptance and need... some to realms greater, other entities perhaps to a bit lesser realms in terms of the fullest potential possible in spiritual form but, nonetheless, free of the Earth and its bonds which previously limited them.

Most all are greeted by those who have loved them or have been with them in the just-previous life or others before this. All are met by great beings of God's love and Light, and they are showered with this Light which heals and purifies and renews them. Most all are transformed in one way or another, arriving at a state of feeling, of thought, and of outward appearance, which is just so more radiant and more healthful and at ease than ever before. For each progression is that which builds upon the light of the previous, and so each is—even though it's perhaps inconceivable in the Earth plane—greater than the previous. See?

The passage of the souls to other realms creates wonder in all those realms associated with the Sea of Faces. There are hundreds, thousands, who often watch at a safe distance with awe, as entities who they have known—perhaps, for many decades or many days or many hours or many minutes— nonetheless, they have known them... and their wonder is a beginning for them, as well.

Example: "How could this one, 'Walter,' who was certainly just as sinful as I, now move into the Light of God? Doesn't he fear? Isn't he ashamed? Doesn't he know he's going to be punished?" and yet all the while, they can see Walter moving, becoming more radiant, his smile and his warmth exuding the energy of love. And perhaps Walter turns to look at them, gesturing, calling them, to come forth and rise with him.

Ceremony of Faith
June 25, 1998

Emotion in the Beyond

The Sea of Faces, generally, denotes differing types of emotional focal points that are predominantly held by the entities therein. Some might be, as you say in the Earth plane, fear-based. Some might be need-based. Others might be guilt-based. And so on and so forth, generally spanning the full array of known emotional definitions, and quite a number that aren't widely known in the Earth.

When one breaks free of this, they are generally free of the dimension in which the Earth is expressed, and we have defined that (on a linear scale) as the Third Realm... or numeric scale, if you will.

So, movement out of finite limitation passes through a sort of inter-dimensional buffer, a sort of (and you've seen this) luminous, gossamer-like space that goes on for, as you would perceive it, some considerable distance as you travel through it—here, again, it is very tiny on the scale of the infinite, see—

to the Fourth Realm and Fifth and Sixth… and most have no capacity to go beyond the Sixth.

In your original question, emotion exists as a potential and as a tool on virtually all levels, all realms of expression.

Work Reading
August 1, 1999

Choosing to Be Lost

The nature of those Forces which are (quote) "lost" (end quote) is not so much so that they are literally lost, but that they choose to be lost. These choices are a part—usually, typically—of those experiences which are the most recent, but not always. There are examples here aplenty. There are those entities who are in the (quote) "Sea of Faces" (end quote) who are there primarily for recurring reasons which have some several thousands of Earth years of historical lineage. These, then, may have been awakened, re-awakened, or brought to the surface by the most just-recent incarnation. So they have fallen back, as they departed from the Earth, into those influences.

All must pass through these in one manner or another, unless they have been left behind. So then, this is like… "crashing into a sea of emotion" that is powerful. If that has been re-awakened, it is like opening a door a bit in self to allow these limiting thoughts to take residence again. See?

Can they depart? In the twinkling of an eye. But theirs is the choice. They must know and believe that they need not do penance any longer… that, as asked in the first moment, so was it given therein.

Work Reading
May 23, 2000

Fueling the Shadowy Forces

The habits, the powers of habit, are fueled by the Forces which could be called shadowy, limiting. How is this possible without an identity, an entity... a "devil"?

It is very simple: It is possible because many entities who are participating in that (we'll call it) mass-mind thought-form are interacting with it continually. It is like a massive chorus, where many voices come together to create a secondary sound, which, for the most part, is heard as a collage of sound, rather than a single voice.

So, with the shadowy forces of habit and limitation (and not all habits are limiting, see, but can be) these, then, the thoughts and the desires of those who are a part of that particular type of shadowy thought-form are continually fueling all of those who are a part of it.

In the instance of those who are dis-eased, this dis-ease is because of a collective way of thinking or habit. Collective from where? (For some are children.) Obviously, from past lives and previous incarnations... in other realms, in other dimensions, as well as the Earth.

These are points of powerful potential for these souls, so powerful, that they manifest in a way which is outstandingly unique—not just a withered limb, lost sight, diminished hearing, a dis-ease to the digestive, or on and on, but the total (seemingly, at least) subjugation of their conscious will to the shadowy forces. See? When there are those conditions of dis-ease and/or limitation which have become so familiar to the one who is dis-eased, a sort of spiritual, mental, and emotional callus forms.

Remember your physical bodies. If you do a certain work that causes abrasion, pressure, continual stress or duress upon some part of the body—let's say the hands, for example, for that's the most common—then the body responds by building up reserve tissues. It builds layer upon layer to form a callus. The skin hardens, toughens, and is more tolerant of the continual challenge made to it.

As above, so is it below; as below, so is it above. The spirit, then, under a continual duress, the emotion battered continually by the same forces, builds a callus and becomes more and more oblivious to those forces, so that they can take a sort of semi-permanent residency in that person's life. The *callus* actually becomes a part of the perpetuation of the dis-ease. Now, remember, we are speaking here of a protective mechanism to the emotion, to the mind, to the heart, see; and so, the condition of limitation manifests in the physical body.

So the Master, or you, can look for this: Where is the tolerance, where is the entry point, that this dis-ease has found its way into the physical body? You might be able to see it in the energy fields around the physical body, if you have allowed yourself the higher sight.

Notice the wording: ...*If you have allowed yourself higher sight.* When we use the word *see*, we are not referring to physical sight. We are referring to all sight, which can include, of course, literal seeing of the aura, the energy fields, and such; but perhaps even more important than this is the capacity to feel it, to know it, and to do so to such an affinity (without claiming it, without sharing in it) that you can not only identify it but take command over it.

These forces know the Light very well. They will know of your coming and your intention, even (notice this) even before you do. They know of the intention of the host, the entity who is dis-eased by their presence, who are about to seek healing. They will fortify in any way possible in advance of that request. They will put forth buffers, veils, things to confuse you, to mislead you, all manner of such, for the Earth is where they dwell.

Of course, God and God's Spirit is life and the foundation upon which the Earth rests. But God's Spirit is the epitome of loving neutrality, a father-mother who knows that their children learn through doing, through experiencing, through interacting. It is so beautiful, so wonderful. When you know it and claim it, then you will see these deceptions, these veils, these buffers, these illusions, that the shadowy forces try to impart.

Remember, they are very familiar with the Earth. It is who and what they are. It is their realm of expression. These shadowy forces cannot move up to the higher realms, and this creates the Sea of Faces: the limited realms beyond the finite, the incarnate, expression of the Earth.

You might ask, then, how does it manifest that we know of other realms, non-physical, wherein limitation exists? Now you have found a key of empowerment, of wisdom. It is this mechanism that perpetuates karma, remembering karma to be the *opportunity*... neither good nor bad. Actually, karma is lovingly neutral. The entity who bears the karma determines its direction—positive or negative.

So look you here: An entity twenty lifetimes past has carried a remorse with them upon passing through the veil separating the Earth from other realms of expression, the doorway, the portal you call death. They carry this to another place, another consciousness. Because it is limiting, they cannot carry it to, let us say, the next Major Realm of expression, which is light-filled. For it cannot exist there. See? Not in that form. So they must go to a realm of familiarity, a sort of symbiotic relationship where entities of like-mind can dwell and experience their common limitation.

In this case, let us say the entity has remorse for a misdeed of their own action. They come back to the Earth when it is appropriate, carrying the seeds of this remorse. And they might do so for those twenty lifetimes! And now, in this, the twenty-first, the seeds bear fruit, because the (quote) "soil of the Earth" (end quote) is appropriate to nourish those seeds once again. Perhaps the same entities who were transgressed against, that predicated the remorse of this soul, are here again, and so all the entities involved are presented with an opportunity to release these limitations. For this entity is the perpetuator and has remorse, and the others might be the victims or the recipients of some misdeed, and perhaps they hold anger or even hatred, and they know not why. See? This powerful key then

81

enables you to not only free that one who has come before thee seeking, but to free many.

Jesus Heals – Part II

December 8, 1999

Part Three:

Joyful Passage

LAMA SING COMMENTARY

To all of you who mourn, let your hearts be gladdened in what shall be given. To all of you who have anger and who seek out to retaliate in kind, our prayers are with you. Yet even so as God's Law is perfect and immutable, so is it then that we honor the Earth and those upon it, for all are our brothers and sisters, and in the righteousness of those who seek to direct and guide, those who desire to lead and establish the principles of goodness and peace, we are with you.

To those who are dwelling in illusion or separateness, hear our call... The Light comes. For those of you who have been a part of certain works which have gone before, we reach out to you, and offer this understanding, and prayerfully so, ask that it inspire you all the greater:

Perhaps as you will recall, those of you who journeyed with us through the experiences of a man whom we call Peter, you, for the better, understand the process and the opportunities which lie beyond.

Perhaps those who might come to know of this shall also find a bit of comfort or reassurance. But for those of you who have walked with us in those works, we take a moment to honor you, every one, and the gift that, together, you have given to the Earth. For, imagine that all those who have of recent Earth hours, and even yet as we speak, are departing the Earth. Imagine that they might behold a glorious Bridge of Light[5], re-

---

[5] Bridge of Light - In a "Peter" reading in 2000, it was requested of those on Earth who were following the Peter journey, that they envision, and literally create through mind and spirit/intention, a Bridge of Light, upon which those departing the Earth Realm could find their way to life beyond with greater ease, literally spanning the Sea of Faces. (Note -The Sea of Faces includes not only those realms that might be considered "evil", but also realms of very benevolent and loving souls who created/became a part of realms of consciousness/habit/desire near to their hearts, such as a "Preachers' Realm".)

splendent with the very beauties of the faithful, drawn from their hearts and minds from that which they have found and called to be good… all of which might have been constructed that their passage from the Earth to the infinite might be one of radiance and beauty.

Perhaps along the Bridge's pathway, there might be those who have gone before and bear the Light—in song, in greeting, in embrace, in prayer—unto every need, a greater measure than is asked. Imagine if that Bridge could connect to a Realm wherein the beauty of each entity's needs would be met and surpassed. And imagine if you had so done (which, of course, you have)… Look at these things, and know them for the goodness, the beauty, and the service in God's name which you have given to those who journey beyond.

$\sim\!\!\!\checkmark$

A STORY OF COMPASSION

A solitary figure is seen weeping, kneeling, hands covering his face. He is approximately mid to late 20's, Earth-age. He is not of the following who are called Christians. He is, in fact, one of the perpetrators of this action perpetuated earlier in your Earth day.

Why is he kneeling? Why is he weeping? Because he is upon the pathway being trod by many souls, many souls whose lives have ended in the physical and have begun in spirit. And he has met, and been challenged by, many different forces.

When he discovered that this was not, as he was told—an act that would lead him on to paradise—but rather that he was greeted by great throngs from the darkness, calling out in various ways unimaginable, the terror in his spirit grew to such dimension that here he is, kneeling, weeping, as he watches those souls pass by whose Earth lives have ended because of his action.

No songs of praise. No ceremonies of rejoicing. Only equal in kind… the messages of the darkness, the voices that choose to separate and divide… voices which perpetuate the desire for power and dominance and hatred, using the weapons of fear, and such as these.

Here and there, he pauses to look up, calling out to them, his hand reaching, grasping, asking, "Forgive me."

It is not that they cannot find in their spirits, many of them, the ability to answer this lad (actually young in heart and mind); it is that they see him not. It is that he is veiled by the separateness of those who surround him. Soon those veils will part, for as he calls out to these individuals passing by, ultimately we know he will ask of God for forgiveness. And we shall answer; the darkness shall fall away, and we shall lead him to his journey's end.

We ask you to look upon this one in the moment of your sadness, your grief, your shock, your disbelief. Not he alone, but the others who were, like him, believers unto the word they were given, and to the promise they believe with all of their being.

It is true that the law of your lands is honored and is, to the greater extent, based upon righteousness. But until such as those principles which nourish—those principles which seek to give birth to a new way of life, a new way of thinking, a new way of living—until this can manifest and be embraced, seen for the wonder of its gift and the power to answer the need so long present in the Earth, then this one pleading with the line of entities passing by, moving up, individually and severally, great tunnels of light, surrounded by those of the very host of God's angelic beings and many of our grouping as well, yet they hear him not

Look you, one and all, *we pray of you,* to the Earth through the eyes of God...

Is it such that distance separates you? Is it because one man might call God Allah and another Jehovah and another by, simply, God, and on and on, that this could so divide and separate that you come to believe they are non-believers; that one path is *the* path, alone, and that the hearts of those who follow a different name, different teachings and yet one truth, are such that they cannot be your brother or sister?

Every entity upon the Earth in this moment as we speak through this, our Channel shall one day come to pass through these veils of separateness. Upon such an occasion, will it be to lament? Will it be to call out for forgiveness? Or will it be with the gladness of one's spirit as thou art surrounded by wondrous, loving, beings, embraced as you move along a pathway of light, glorified in the color and music of the spheres?

No one shall enter into the kingdom of God without their spirits being awakened. One cannot awaken their spirit when it is burdened, when it is in the sleep of illusion and habit.

It is only as one seeks to know and claim, and to become that which they hold to be righteous within, that the Way can truly be open and passable, and that they can enter in to the kingdom of God. But it is not the doorway called *Death* that awaits you for entry into the kingdoms of God... only your choice... only your wish... your prayer... and your willingness to release that which impedes or limits you; that, having so done, all that is a part of the Promise is, in the very next moment, yours to claim.

As we look upon this young man one final time, we can tell you that the agony, the pain, the fear, the sense of betrayal and the sense of no reference, are beyond imagination and our capacity to express in your words. It is not God who places these upon him nor even the thoughts of the many-fold of the Earth who direct anger and hatred towards the perpetrators, but he, himself... fueled by those in the darkness who find some curious accomplishment by nourishing these thoughts of pain and agony.

So we would ask of you, remember them in prayer, as well. If you call yourself a follower of the Master, the Christ, then you must test your thinking. Mustn't you?

For here is the message from our Lord:

I AM The Light and The Way. Those who cleave unto me and my Word, cleave unto the Promise of God. For it is His Word that I speak, and it is the womb of God that bears His grace. For the creative aspect of our Lord God must be seen equal to that which can give life in any and all realms.

Love and Compassion are the step-stones unto the kingdom within. For lest you find these Principles distant, then so art thou distant, as well.

So then, dear friends, as we turn to conclude here, it is appropriate and honorable that we should mention in thankfulness a special blessing for those of you who have gone forth into the darkness repeatedly to answer those calls as come from same. We glorify you, for you are servants of the Light. You do bear the love and compassion of God's Promise; that Grace is ever yours.

You will find many have been lost by the Darkness this day; many souls have turned away from limitation, and those forces as would dominate them. Even as we are speaking, beautiful souls are gathering them up. Those of you who been a part of these works, reflect on this, and rejoice in it. The power of God's Word is awakened within them, and naught that the Darkness can offer to them in the form of challenge can diminish the gentle Light within. It is the Promise of God, known again, and it brings Light to the Darkness.

As we conclude here, we offer this prayer to you, and we encourage you to celebrate *each moment* of your life… These are as gifts of opportunity and of hopefulness, and you might oft think of yourselves as instruments of God, so as you choose. The power which awaits you has always been yours. Now is the time. The great cycles of the folding and undulating movements of time and space (as you call it) have come back together again. In the passage of these, you shall find that the Promise will manifest—and He shall come.

O Father-Mother God we pray unto Thee on behalf of all those who might hear our words. Let their hearts and spirits be open. Let them transcend limitation or the impression of separateness. Let them go beyond the divisions of caste or faith, or the divisions of male and female, or those who have of greatness of the Earth's abundance and those who have little. Let them go beyond the illusion of the appearance of their bodies physical and let them see the beauty of each spirit which dwells within same. As we, their brethren, Lord God, ask it of Thee, we do so in the name of the Master, the Christ.

So, too, do we offer this prayer of hope and promise unto those who are "lost," Thy Word, the promise of joyful expectancy: We call upon you. Come. Join us. We await you.

But our prayer, Lord God, is for Thy faithful in Earth, first and foremost. Let their hearts rejoice in the face of challenge, of sadness, of hardship, that they might ever remember that Thou art their God.

So let be written.

Fare thee well then for the present, dear friends. Om Shanti.

THE REST OF THE STORY:

A MESSAGE FROM THE ELDERS

We have paused the Channel in his return to the Earth, that we might offer in this commentary of explanation for those who are willing to hear same. In that given above, it was shared that one young man in his mid to late 20's, Earth-time measure, was pleading for forgiveness. What was not given and which might seem to be curious is the following:

Upon his passage through the portal called death he continued on, believing that the impact had not yet taken place. When he realized that he was still in existence in the manner that he would know to be similar to that of the Earth, he called out unto his God.

As the illusion of the surroundings just previous to the impact faded, he found himself standing in an open place, alone. Though there were messengers of God present—his guides, if you will—he could see them not, for his spirit was not open to see. The Law is perfect; and in order to pass from one realm of consciousness to that which lies beyond—to ascend, so to say, or to move into the Light, as it is so often called in the Earth— one must meet that which has been the journey being left behind. Thus this man saw the lifetimes of *each entity* whose (as you call it) death was a result of his action. He saw their lifetimes from birth through childhood. He saw each event of joy, of sorrow. He saw their families... and knew them... and felt the love and the compassion. He felt the frustrations. He felt it all. He heard the lamentations of those left behind. He felt their emotion. And, finally, he saw them, as they passed by.

An eternity of such events transpired in mere Earth hours. Each soul was visited in this manner; each soul is now known to him. And in his spirit's heart, he knows the Law, and he feels the burden of what you call Karma.

It is not that this small commentary as an addendum is

meant to imply anything, but only to clarify. For when he does realize that forgiveness is offered by God, we can embrace him and we shall. It will not be the end for him. We can move him from his position within the shadows, or the darkness, as he asks it. Perhaps in a time, he will come to a state of understanding and he will choose—as others before, perhaps even some of you who are hearing these words—that he might journey in the quest of his own spirit once again.

He has lived the measure of an eternity, steeped in the emotion that is imaginable or expected from within same. He is feeling the thoughts and attitudes of those who are left behind, orphaned, widowed. And he is feeling the anger and hatred of that which he thought to be holy, that which he thought to be a work in the name of the God that he was taught he might expect.

It is true… When he looks down at his hands as the instruments of his will—that they directed the death of so many—and as he cries out, "O Allah, wrest them from my body, that never again shall I commit such an action of such a nature!"—perhaps, because his belief in this is strong, he will in time return to the Earth without the use of his hands and arms. If he does so, as is quite likely in the present, he will come to discover that it is the spirit, the will, the mind, the heart, that doeth the work, just so as to those who commanded him, used him.

We thank you for permitting us this brief commentary, and it is our prayer in that it shall be of further clarification. We are called the Elders. We are with you and Our Lady. We ask those of you who can hear and see to begin your journey *now*. Look you well, could there be a better time? We call upon the blessings and grace of God to ever surround and embrace you. Fare thee well, then, for the present, dear friends.

Journey of Compassion
September 11, 2001

READING 6: 9/11 REVISITED

LAMA SING COMMENTARY

Here we walk before all these beautiful souls who have gathered, in a manner of speaking, to celebrate their movement from finiteness into the infinite embrace of the tenets of God.

As we move throughout the groupings as they are gathered, some, we notice, stand in a shadowy place. Their appearance, their demeanor, their faces if you will, demonstrative of that which is within and which limits.

A GARDEN OF LIGHT

Now we move on to that place where there is the brightness of the sun's light, as you would know it. The azure, incredible depth of a sky above is filled with the expected beautiful white clouds, the greenery undulating in its vibrancy all about, lovely paths, benches, arbors, small knolls, little reflection pools, cascading waterfalls, the song of birds in flight joyfully calling out to the sons and daughters of God.

Here, we look upon one, and the next, and we see the radiance in their faces. We see their countenance glowing with the vibrancy of that which they have claimed, and taken unto themselves.

Below them, in the shadows, their brothers and sisters who cannot accept... who do not know in the truth of their being that they are called to move on, to traverse the temptation, the shadows of darkness, the deceptive Forces of habit and denial, the imposition of self-judgment and guilt and the diminished capacity to forgive themselves... thereafter, of course, the holding of those thoughts which lack forgiveness for others.

So, of course, we choose to stand beside our brothers and sisters who are in the light, in this garden of their own creation, beautiful, as they the creators have so brought it about. The freedom of their spirits echoes as an energy which embraces you merely by being present with them. Their thought is as an incredibly enchanting song of pure joy.

Who are these beings? And why is their light so great, so endearing? Why does it call out so powerfully, to the contrast to those who have gone within, to dwell there as their choice?

One Year Later...

In this day in the Earth plane there are many who hold an array of thoughts that go well beyond that which we have humbly attempted to convey using mere words. Yet, as some of you would look upon these scenes—broadcast through the television, announced via the radio waves and so forth, and borne in the printed word—where are *you* as you witness these things in Earth? From whence do you see them... this beautiful Garden of Light, or in the shadowy recesses of limitation?

Hold you, yet, hatred, anger, and a desire for vengeance against those who have perpetuated this great loss? Are you among those who call out from your hearts for retribution? Are the balance scales of justice tipped in your mind, heart, and intent? If any of these are so, then the shadows belong to you. The shadows will embrace you because those are the thoughts that the shadows embrace. The power of the Forces of Limitation seek not to sing out with joy, but rather with false pride, false ego, and power. They call to you just as strongly perhaps as do the sons and daughters who have created this realm of beauty... and who have done so i*n the face of the same event!*

Is it your decision, then...

That you shall continue upon a pathway that divides and separates you from the oneness of the light these sweet souls have made manifest in the hope and prayer that it will shine down upon you and give you comfort, bring you the reassurance that yet they exist and to the greater joy than many can ever find in Earth because the heart is unwilling.

If you walk upon a pathway in the Earth plane and you give it power through your thought and intention, haven't you, in those very actions, created the destination unto which *you* will arrive at journey's end? If it is the power of God that you truly seek, if it is Oneness with God and the manifestation of those times of jubilation in the Earth you desire, what is your contribution unto that?

For it is of profound Truth that the Earth is the Realm of those souls who have chosen to dwell therein and upon; and that their choice has so manifested, then, that now they are at the ready to manifest according to their intent, to their desire, in the full potential of God. For that intent and desire *is* the Earth, and will be the future for it if changes are not made.

So... here are we, in the midst of the many here, whose faces are familiar to those of you who loved them while they were in the Earth, whose hearts are even purer, whose qualities of goodness are amplified beyond that which you have known in the Earth. Here, then, are they, come unto your events of this Earth day to softly, gently, offer to you that which they have: "Forgive them. For, in truth, they have known not what they have done. Free their spirits from the bondage of your hatred, your remorse, your sadness, your anger, for that is the only way you can free yourself, as well."

You can ask anyone here... and we shall, in a moment ahead, do just that... but, you can ask any of them, and we are quite certain that their answer will be some variation upon the same general theme.

Our question of them would be, as it shall just ahead: "What has brought you to this place of profound beauty and light, while we look down only a distance away, separated by veils of illusion, and there are others whose lot was the same as yours yet who now dwell in the shadows... who struggle to find purpose, meaning... who are devoid of one whit of the magnitude of joy, love, and compassion that permeate every aspect of this beautiful realm of your creation?"

So we ask them the question, "Sir? How have you come to be in this place? How have you come to find the joy and happiness that is so evident, radiating from you as we stand before you?"

95

The one we stand before would be measured in your Earth age perhaps late thirties-early forties... one of the many workers in those Twin Towers... one who turned to see what that sound was, and saw and felt the impact of it... among the first who did.

"And so, sir, to what would you point to, that has freed you?"

He gestures us to come, here, to a beautiful geometric design upon the ground... a mosaic, the patterns are enchanting... and he gestures for us to seat ourselves, as he so does, upon a lustrous white, marble-like bench, intricately engraved work of passion from the heart of its joyful creator.

And now we repeat his words, as best we can, our prayer going before them, that we could, so humbly, truly honor the magnificence of this son of God:

$$\smile\!\!/$$

ONE MAN'S JOURNEY

The Net Of Illusion

While I was in the Earth, and looked with shock to see the craft and then a blinding moment or two, and I looked around and could see naught that was familiar, I felt a strong energy, pulling on me... and another pulling in another direction.

I looked about, and I saw naught but darkness, and for a moment a thought of fear and panic visited me. But something embraced me from the darkness. I knew it not, and yet, within me, I realized I have always known it.

I saw, then, that the fear, the doubt, the sense of not knowing where I was, or what I was, for that matter, was seen through the eyes of eternity... *my* eternity. I saw it to be like a covering, like a mesh of some sort of woven intent pulling me off to the side. Somehow, I reached up and took it down from my being, and dropped it. I looked at it. It had a strange, curious, luminosity and essence that possessed some energy, like a

96

dull light, throbbing currents of different forces, which I saw as colors and such, pulsing all throughout the weave of the net.

A shudder went through my being, for I knew in that moment, *it wanted me!* Again and again it tried to come to life and to encompass me again. But I found I merely had to look at it and know it for its meaning, its being, and it was powerless.

After a time of studying this, I looked about again.

The Call

Now the darkness seemed rich and warm somehow; not like the darkness of a black curtain, but as the inviting call of all that has been and all that can be, calling out to me to come.

The call was so great and, like an echo deep within me, I heard the call answered, and I found a sense of peace and joy. In that state, I let go of it all. I saw the great net of illusion falling away, far behind. I felt myself soaring… and I felt the goodness and the peace.

I contemplated what had just been and, as I did, I saw all those with whom I had walked upon the journey of this lifetime. I stirred deep within as I looked into the faces and eyes, smiling at me, of all those I had loved during this journey.

Remembering Paths

Then, I saw many other faces, and I remembered, with incredible detail, how my journey had woven itself into theirs. How our paths had crossed. How we attempted to tell each other of our thoughts, our hopes, our desires; but the net of illusion was so strong upon us—the words we spoke, the actions we perpetuated of the Earth so familiar, powerful in their habit and lure of the familiar—that in the moment of revisiting each of these in magnificent detail, I came to see that the message that we wanted to convey to each other was never as it was meant to be from our heart. Rather, the message was distorted by that which we believed to be the only truth, the only reality.

I felt a pang of sadness as I saw this one, and that, and another, who, from this point in my journey, I recognized with joy as an old friend, a sister from somewhere in the depths of the majestic darkness, yet while in my life on Earth, I had known them not.

Then, something passed through me and conveyed to me the thought that said to me, "That's alright. You can visit them again. They will come and join you in their time, when they are prepared. Journey on now and leave them with the embrace of your knowledge of who and what they *truly* are. And release them, that *their* journey might continue, and the time of reunion can be just that much swifter."

Resisting the Lure

In contrast to the Earth I found this very easy to do. I suppose because, as I tried it, there was such a good feeling of peace... a sense of expectancy and hope... the understanding that this is but a journey and, when it concludes, we will come together and perhaps journey onward arm-in-arm, this time, knowing that we are brother and sister, or friends.

I saw all the faces of each one I had met in my journey through life just behind me, and I gave unto them, as it was now being given to me, love. I found small tweaks and twinges here and there where an adjudged wrong from the Earth perspective pulled at me. But the vision of that ugly net of heavy, muted colors, quickly reminded me: I can choose to be free; or I can choose to hold onto this thought of having been wronged and call out unto the righteousness of what is for the righting of that wrong, for the pound of flesh for the pound of flesh taken.

As I contemplated that, just a moment or two, I could feel its call to me, saying, "There is righteousness for you *here*. You can have your balance. You can receive your just dues. They have wronged you. Claim the right to reciprocate."

There was a heaviness that came with all of these offers, all of these subtle calls... gentle... beckoning... summoning me to join them and to stop my journey into what was unknown.

I looked upon these choices. I looked at all that had been.

Then, I felt this inner call answering the one from beyond, and I laughed aloud with joy! *I laughed!* Because I had seen the face of illusion, heard its call. Now I chose to see the face of God... to hear God's words... God's call.

The instant I so did, my journey resumed, and I realized that I had moved through something that had the power to call me aside, to give to me a different life... a life of familiarity and habit, a life which offered an eye for an eye, continual *getting even.*

The first that I saw dazzled me in her beauty. She was veritably made of light and yet I could see her form. Like any one of you in the Earth, who might hear these words, I might have so seen you, just the same. Her face was gentle, soft, smiling. Her hair cascaded down. Her form had definition from above, and, as my gaze followed downward, began to dissipate. The garment was flowing, like a living light, but so much more.

As I looked upon her garment, it seemed that small portion of it *knew* I was perceiving it and radiated all the more. The colors, and sounds, and expressions... I have no words from the Earth to use here, except to say that it made me feel good and joyful. She came from slightly above, out of the darkness, like the birth of a light; and the form, as it became more defined, reached out to me.

Reviewing the Past

For a moment or two, I hesitated. You might ask, why?

I suppose my hesitation was in part due to several different things, but collectively I would sum them to say because of habit and perhaps the feeling of being unworthy.

Then, for another moment (which might be measured as much longer than that), I thought of all those I loved and whose love I could still feel. What will they do without me, and I, them? I looked into her face... her eyes gentle, loving, sweet... and I thought about all the things I had done and experienced, things I had participated in, even though I knew them not to be just so proper; and I looked at her again, thinking, in that instant, she too must have seen them, and perhaps now she would turn away, as my thought of them gave them life, so to say.

But she did not. In fact, it seemed the sweetness of her smile, and the unwavering presence of her outstretched hand became even more beautiful, more luminous and bright, more clearly defined.

Then I heard a voice say, "It is your choice. We call to you to join us. We ask you to free yourself and to move beyond that which still calls out to you."

I looked about in amazement and saw naught but this beautiful lady before me. I could perceive no movement of her lips, and I thought, "Surely this is an angel of God. But who speaks to me? Is it she?" all the while her lovely gaze, so sweet, fixed upon me, as a light focuses upon an object in the darkness.

A wave of something passed through me… and another… each one as a grand and glorious color, powerful in its purity and beauty… each one stimulating within me, where, I knew not, for I knew not of what I was but I knew I was… all of the colors of the Earth, one after another, powerful and then yielding to the embrace of the next, merging together, and the next color and the next. With the passage of each of these, I saw the truth of my previous journey in life. I saw the meaning of each experience—those I had released and those that still had some essence, some connection to me—and the light helped me to understand and release those.

Journeying Beyond, Until…

Finally, the last and greatest of the lights came. When it passed, I felt unlike anything I could recall from my previous life, and there I was, in the darkness again, as though suspended in an evening sky void of any celestial light.

I felt the stillness. I felt the peace. I knew that I could remain like this. From somewhere, this knowledge came to me, and it felt good. I dwelled that way for a time, reflecting, pondering where this beautiful angelic being had gone. There was a subtle thought that came to me, "Perhaps I had erred somehow," and the peace simply dissolved the thought, for I knew it was not so. I finally came to know that it was but a thought away... my thought... my *choice*.

So I summoned the thought forth and held it only a brief instant, and she reappeared before me. I took her hand, and we journeyed a glorious journey. We soared through the heavens and so much more. I looked upon many things... of diversity, of beauty and charm, of substance beyond that I had ever known in Earth. I looked upon the faces and the creations they had made. As I looked upon these faces, I knew them. I knew what brought them joy, for it was that which they had created.

The angel looked at me, and I knew she asked, "Would you choose this?"

Carefully, I looked. I saw beautiful things. I saw them in forms just so the same as the physical body I had just left behind, and with the patience of eternity, her smile continued as she awaited my answer.

Again and again I softly said, "It is beautiful, but, no... I would journey with you beyond this. Thank you for the offering of it to me."

On and on we journeyed, through untold expressions, created by those who had gathered around those thoughts, embraced obviously by the sense of... perhaps I might call it joy, that the dwelling in those creations gave unto those who were the inhabitants of same, each somehow mystically separated by some wondrous essence of a substance and form like light in the Earth but living, moving, pulsing with dimensions and magnitudes of hues and colors and such; and beyond it, another place, and other people focused upon where they were and what they were doing. Obviously, this is where they wanted to be. None saw me or the angel with me as we passed through, even though I could reach out and touch them if I had so desired. That close was I, and they saw me not.

And yet we moved. And moved.

Sometimes I felt curious feelings as we would enter new realms of creation and observe those who dwelled there. They were much like feelings in the Earth. The memories of those feelings seemed to be the living essence of which these realms were created. And I mused to myself, "They are reliving this memory." I would look at the angel, and she would nod and smile, affirming my thought.

So I came to understand… so clearly, so beautifully… that each new realm of creation or expression was like a nucleus around which they soared, moved, lived, and believed; and that, for so long as that was their choice and joy, they would stay there. I came to understand that I could choose any one of these and be with them and that I would be warmly embraced, made to feel one of them for so long as I held to the core thought, the nucleus of this realm's very existence.

I would like to tell you that, often, some were so appealing that I tested it against something within me. As I did, I found it to be not quite right, not quite the completeness that I was now beginning to realize was of *my* choice and my choice alone. That is when I realized that I wasn't going to now endure something that was the result of my life just passed (good, bad, or indifferent), but that I could choose my destination.

I also realized that, had I understood this more completely while in my life on Earth, I could have chosen any one of many other paths at any time. The freedom and joy and exhilaration that I was now feeling, with this beautiful lady at my side, was also offered to me *every step of the way while I was in that body in Earth!* It had such an impact on me, that we had to stop, and she comforted me in ways that I still don't remember. Somehow, she brought forth a light or something and placed it around me, and it felt good. I released my feelings and, as I saw them floating away… just like so many had done when I passed through the beautiful colors, I saw these floating down, drifting down, back to the realms in which they belonged.

Then I knew… All of it, *everything*, is a question of choice.

There was the subtle memory—even though they were so far below, yet did I feel the subtlety—of those whose lot in life on Earth is burdened so upon entry, their bodies deformed, or born into a society filled with hunger, pain, disease, hatred, war. I turned to look into the eyes of this beautiful being next to me, and I saw the answers in her eyes, "Yes... they have chosen it." Perhaps returning to the Earth from the shadowy lower realms that I passed through, hoping to wake up and understand that *they choose it... that everyone chooses it!* It is the fruits of the chosen, sown into the actions of life, upon which in the years that follow all must dine.

A curious shiver went through me... call it a shiver of truth, a shiver of understanding... and I shed the last vestiges, as best I know, of that which was impeding me. The moment I did, my journey resumed.

Much more transpired, but I would summarize for you that, ultimately, I came to meet others... Look around. Here they are. More than these come and go, and they embrace us and tell us that even greater than this lies beyond and that, when we are ready, we can choose that, as well.

So if you would ask me, "Why don't you just choose it now?" well, I can tell you, don't think I hadn't thought of that. Often. But remember when I told you about the call I heard off in the distance, right near the beginning of my journey? And how I felt something deep inside me like an echo respond to that call? Well, I'm working on that echo part of myself, because I know the call, the echo that I felt, heard, experienced, deep within me, is what we call God.

So as I look around here, I'm not in a hurry to move on. It's rather like being presented a very beautiful gift and being told there are other gifts after it; for now, I want to enjoy this gift.

To You Yet On Earth

I suppose you can tell, from what's been recounted to you that I and the others have come here today to talk to you about this in the midst of all the events of varying types and nature in the Earth, your current Earth day one year after my departure... those of us who have chosen to be free wanted to share this with you. I wasn't actually chosen, but I asked if I could speak, and the others are so sweet they all agreed. But it's not just me, for my story and theirs are nearly the same, subtle differences that make up our unique individualities... which, by the way, are even more powerful and more beautiful now than they were on Earth (not to digress here, but, maybe it will be of some value).

In the Earth plane, some strut about, believing that they have power and authority and that this makes them important, but the least among you is equal to the greatest. For God has created the beauty in His Word, and that is *each one of you!*

And that is a key, a key which can unlock the destiny of Earth: that you don't have to compete for worthiness; you don't have to compete to be of value, to have a gift to give. But you do have to want the gift. And in the wanting, you have to be willing to release that which is like that sticky net I told you about at the beginning of my journey.

So, to all of you... I could tell you that we send our prayers to you. You'd hear that, and maybe say something appropriate, like, "Oh, how wonderful," or "Oh, I knew it was that way," but I also know that probably tomorrow or the next day you'd forget all about it. I could tell you many of the things that others have told and are telling you even now... how to claim all this and even greater, how to be free. But don't you really already know this? I did. And I chose the other. I didn't do too badly, in the measure of things on Earth. But from here, I did wonderfully! And here I am—free, as testimony, because I could forgive myself and others.

The net of illusion and habit and familiarity, the pallet of emotional colors with which I could have painted my thoughts, are in their rightful place: a part of the experiences which are gifts to each who would take of them and grow, and which becomes the net of limitation for those who take of them and do not grow. So we'd like to, collectively, leave you with a few little thoughts:

You can believe this discourse, or not. It's your choice.

You can believe in the things in Earth that are holding you back, limiting you, distracting you. That is also your choice.

Or you could try, in the moments or minutes or days that follow, changing a few little things…

…in how you think,

…in what you feel,

…in the words that you speak,

…and in the creative actions, that you give to the Earth.

And see what happens…

If you find it to produce something good… you know, if you feel a little better, or your body doesn't hurt quite like it did, or your mind is clearer, anything… if you look for the signs of the result of changing your thinking and actions and you see them to be the slightest bit better, wouldn't you want to go a bit further? Try a bit of kindness where it isn't sought, where it is not deserved. Try to forgive someone who transgresses against you in any way. See how that feels. See what that produces. Because, after all, as that fellow said… the one[6] in that place in Virginia Beach… "Mind is," after all, "the builder."

A CLOSING COMMENT FROM THE GUEST SPEAKER

Forgiveness is the gift offered to you, on this day of remembrance of my departure from Earth: If you can express forgiveness, that is the memorial we would relish most from you on Earth.

We… [continuing choked pauses] …love… you… all.

---

[6]Fellow in Virginia Beach – referring to Edgar Cayce

CLOSING COMMENTS

It is difficult in the consciousness of Earth to know the nature of the light that shines in that which gives life in each entity. Without having walked through the portals, without having trod the footsteps that that soul has trod, how can one truly know of how they have become who and what they are? If the product of their intent and the energies of their thoughts, words, and deeds, are those of hatred, from which seed has this come? For all who know and love God know that His seed is good.

Then it must be those who have fashioned the fruit of God's seed into that which has fulfilled their intent or desire, that such illusions of limitations, such distortions of God's Word, have come to be believed on the part of those whom you see. Those who perpetrated such acts were those who were filled with hatred, but it was their hatred of that which they believed defiled God, the power of that hatred, such that they were (and many yet are) willing to give all in His name to purify their God.

Many have given their lives in a holy cause or work. And here they are. They have recognized that that path has borne only fruits like in kind to that which they have sown— that hatred has begot hatred, that anger has brought them anger in return. Their sadness, their sense of frustration and futility, might be the very keys which free them from the previous illusion.

Here stand the little child and her mother whose lives were taken, who knew not that morn as they embarked upon their journey, that the journey would be one into eternity... here they are, the mother and child, to give this message to those of you who are willing to hear it:

"God is love, and we are of God... God's Children. We have given that which you see as our lives on Earth in service to God and as an expression of our own love for you all.

"In your heart, where there has been grief, let joy come in. In your hearts, where there has been anger and the wish for retribution, let understanding and compassion now become

resident. Where you have had fear, let the certainty of the conti-
nuity of life eternal, through our words, embrace you now and
always.

"Build your hearts as a living temple unto the truth and
eternal nature of God.

"Summon all that you are and all that you believe into
this one work... the work of forgiveness."

911 Revisited
September 11, 2000

About Lama Sing

More than thirty years ago, for our convenience, the one through whom this information flows accepted the name Lama Sing, though it was stated they, themselves, have no need for names or titles.

"We identify ourselves only as servants of God, dedicated to you, our brothers and sisters in the Earth." –Lama Sing

About This Channel

"Channel is that term given generally to those who enable themselves to be, as much as possible, open and passable in terms of information that can pass through them from the Universal Consciousness or other such which are not associated in the direct sense with their finite consciousness of the current incarnation." –Lama Sing

BOOKS BY AL MINER & LAMA SING

The Chosen: Backstory to the Essene Legacy
The Promise: Book I of The Essene Legacy
The Awakening: Book II of The Essene Legacy
The Path: Book III of The Essene Legacy

In Realms Beyond: Book I of The Peter Chronicles
In Realms Beyond: Study Guide
Awakening Hope: Book II of The Peter Chronicles
Return to Earth: Book III of The Peter Chronicle

Death, Dying, and Beyond: How to Prepare for The Journey Vol I
The Sea of Faces: How to Prepare for The Journey Vol II

Jesus: Book I
Jesus: Book II

The Course in Mastery

When Comes the Call

Seed Thoughts
Seed Thoughts to Consciousness

Stepstones: Compilation 1

The Children's Story

About Al Miner

A chance hypnosis session in 1973 began Al's tenure as the channel for Lama Sing. Since then, nearly 10,000 readings have been given in a trance state answering technical and personal questions on such topics as science, health and disease, history, geophysical, spiritual, philosophical, metaphysical, past and future times, and much more. The validity of the information has been substantiated and documented by research institutions and individuals, and those receiving personal readings continue to refer others to Al's work based on the accuracy and integrity of the information in their readings. In 1984, St. Johns University awarded Al an honorary doctoral degree in parapsychology.

Al conducts a variety of field research projects, as well as occasional workshops and lectures. He is no longer accepting requests for personal readings, but, rather, is devoting his remaining time to works intended to be good for all. Much of his current research is dedicated to the concept that the best of all guidance is that which comes from within. Al lives with his wife in Florida.